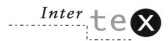

The Language of Politics

'. . . a useful and original resource, with effective and focused class-based activities – invaluable for coursework – the commentaries are particularly helpful.'

Linda Varley, Principal Moderator for Coursework, NEAB,
A-Level English Language, and *Ashton-under-Lyne Sixth Form College*

'This book is written in a very accessible style, with a range of well-chosen examples that will engage the imagination of students and teachers.'

Kay Richardson, *School of Politics and Communications,*
University of Liverpool

This accessible satellite textbook in the Routledge INTERTEXT series is unique in offering students hands-on practical experience of textual analysis focused on the language of politics. Written in a clear, user-friendly style by an experienced writer and teacher, it combines practical activities with texts, accompanied by commentaries which show how language is used by contemporary politicians and how it is part of the wider process of political discourse. There are suggestions for further research and activities. It can be used individually or in conjunction with the series core textbook, *Working with Texts: A core book for language analysis.*

Aimed at A-Level and beginning undergraduate students, *The Language of Politics*:

◎ examines how both politicians and commentators describe political stances
◎ explores some of the most common linguistic features to be found in political speeches
◎ analyses electioneering through various written texts including manifestos, posters and pamphlets
◎ looks at how politicians answer questions both in the media and in parliament
◎ includes examples of political discourse from Britain, America and Australia
◎ has a comprehensive glossary of terms.

Adrian Beard is Head of English at Gosforth High School in Newcastle-upon-Tyne and Principal Moderator at the Northern Examining and Assessment Board for A-Level English Literature. His previous publications include *The Language of Sport* (1998) for the INTERTEXT series.

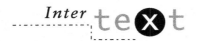

The Intertext series

◎ **Why does the phrase 'spinning a yarn' refer both to using language and making cloth?**

◎ **What might a piece of literary writing have in common with an advert or a note from the milkman?**

◎ **What aspects of language are important to understand when analysing texts?**

The Routledge INTERTEXT series will develop readers' understanding of how texts work. It does this by showing some of the designs and patterns in the language from which they are made, by placing texts within the contexts in which they occur, and by exploring relationships between them.

The series consists of a foundation text, *Working with Texts: A core book for language analysis*, which looks at language aspects essential for the analysis of texts, and a range of satellite texts. These apply aspects of language to a particular topic area in more detail. They complement the core text and can also be used alone, providing the user has the foundation skills furnished by the core text.

Benefits of using this series:

◎ **Unique** – written by a team of respected teachers and practitioners whose ideas and activities have also been trialled independently

◎ **Multi-disciplinary** – provides a foundation for the analysis of texts, supporting students who want to achieve a detailed focus on language

◎ **Accessible** – no previous knowledge of language analysis is assumed, just an interest in language use

◎ **Comprehensive** – wide coverage of different genres: literary texts, notes, memos, signs, advertisements, leaflets, speeches, conversation

◎ **Student-friendly** – contains suggestions for further reading; activities relating to texts studied; commentaries after activities; key terms highlighted and an index of terms

The Language of Politics

- Adrian Beard

ROUTLEDGE
Taylor & Francis Group

First published 2000
by Routledge
2 Park Square, Milton Park,
Abingdon, Oxon, OX14 4RN

Simultaneously published in the USA
and Canada
by Routledge
270 Madison Ave, New York NY 10016

*Routledge is an imprint of the Taylor & Francis
Group*

Transferred to Digital Printing 2010

© 2000 Adrian Beard

Typeset in Stone Sans/Stone Serif by
Solidus (Bristol) Limited

*British Library Cataloguing in Publication
Data*

A catalogue record for this book is
available from the British Library

*Library of Congress Cataloguing in Publication
Data*

Beard, Adrian, 1951–
  The language of politics / Adrian
Beard.
    p. cm. –– (Intertext)
    Includes bibliographical references
  (p.   ) and index.
    ISBN 0–415–20178–0 (pb)
    1 English language––Discourse
analysis. 2. Politicians––English
-speaking countries––Language.
3. Political science––English
-speaking countries––Terminology.
I. Title. II. Series: Intertext
(London, England)
PE1422.B4   2000
420.1'41––dc21   99-23246
                                        CIP

ISBN 0–415–20178–0

The series editors:

Ronald Carter is Professor of Modern English Language in the Department of English Studies at the University of Nottingham and is the editor of the Routledge INTERFACE series in Language and Literary Studies. He is also co-author of *The Routledge History of Literature in English*. From 1989 to 1992 he was seconded as National Director for the Language in the National Curriculum (LINC) project, directing a £21.4 million in-service teacher education programme.

Angela Goddard is Senior Lecturer in Language at the Centre for Human Communication, Manchester Metropolitan University, and was Chief Moderator for the project element of English Language A-Level for the Northern Examination and Assessment Board (NEAB) from 1983 to 1995. Her publications include *The Language Awareness Project: Language and Gender*, vols I and II, 1988, and *Researching Language*, 1993 (Framework Press).

Core textbook:

Working with Texts: A core book for language analysis
Ronald Carter, Angela Goddard, Danuta Reah, Keith Sanger, Maggie Bowring

Satellite titles:

The Language of Sport
Adrian Beard

The Language of Humour
Alison Ross

The Language of Advertising: Written texts
Angela Goddard

The Language of Fiction
Keith Sanger

The Language of Poetry
John McRae

The Language of Politics
Adrian Beard

The Language of Newspapers
Danuta Reah

Language and Gender
Angela Goddard

Related titles:

INTERFACE series:

Variety in Written English
Tony Bex

The Discourse of Advertising
Guy Cook

Language, Literature and Critical Practice
David Birch

Literary Studies in Action
Alan Durant and Nigel Fabb

A Linguistic History of English Poetry
Richard Bradford

English in Speech and Writing
Rebecca Hughes

The Language of Jokes
Delia Chiaro

Feminist Stylistics
Sara Mills

contents

acknowledgements

Thanks to Angela Goddard and Ron Carter for their help and encouragement; to Jean and Harry Beard for the Taunton data; to Gemma Garland at the Australian High Commission for her research and data; to the Labour Party for data; to the Liberal Democrats for data; to US Democrats Abroad for helpful suggestions. Also thanks to the A-Level English students at Gosforth High School, Newcastle-upon-Tyne for their help with trials of some of the material in this book.

The author and publishers wish to thank the following for permission to reprint copyright material:

Hope Pym at *Private Eye* for 'St Albion'; Hansard for British Parliamentary speeches; The Australian High Commission for Australian Parliamentary speeches; Pete Davies and the Tessa Sayle Agency for the extract from *This England*; John Humphrys for 'Tony Blair Interview'; The Labour Party for '1997 Manifesto', 'billboard posters' and 'Tony Blair poster'; The Liberal Democrats for 'End the Punch and Judy Show', 'Hallam News' and 'Somerset Mail'.

introduction

When the British Prime Minister Harold Wilson said 'A week is a long time in politics', he was referring to the fact that political success and failure were never far apart, and that a week could make all the difference either way. His words are equally relevant, though, to the sheer volume of material that is produced each week on political issues. To read, watch and listen to all the political output that the media produce each week would be impossible; we have to read selectively if we are to cope.

This book, although titled *The Language of Politics*, is not claiming to be anything more than an introduction to some of the areas students might wish to research if they are interested in politics. Its data have been selected to illustrate certain broad principles, rather than to allow highly detailed analysis of specific political issues. With so many words produced by politicians and commentators, students rarely experience difficulty finding good contemporary data. What they do sometimes find difficult is knowing what to do with the data, and it is here that this book should help.

The first unit explores some commonly held, and usually negative, perceptions of politics and politicians. It then examines how politicians describe their own political stance, and how others describe it for them, before looking at how satirical writers have attacked political systems and figures.

The second unit focuses on some semantic issues. It looks at the way political discourse uses metaphor, metonymy and analogy, and what this usage says about the political culture that produces it. It also explores the idea of 'spin' and the way all meaning is relative.

The third and fourth units focus on election campaigns. Unit 3 looks at slogans and posters, while Unit 4 analyses political manifestos, local campaigns and press reports.

Unit 5 looks at various aspects of political rhetoric and speeches.

The final unit, Unit 6, analyses the way politicians answer questions, both in parliament and when interviewed in the media.

In *The Language of Politics*, the word 'politics' has been used in a highly specific way - it refers to the democratic systems which provide the governments of most of the economically developed nations of the world. Before beginning the analysis of how language is used in such systems, it is important to note the following:

- Political systems exist which are different from, but not necessarily inferior to, those seen in the world's most economically developed countries.
- Within these economically developed countries there are those who question and challenge the assumptions upon which their political systems are based.
- These systems are called democratic, but are rooted very deeply in traditional power structures, involving issues of gender, race, class and culture.

This means that this book, because it is going to concentrate on the world of professional power politics, is only looking at part of the picture, albeit a significant part. Essentially it is going to look at the language of an occupation - that of the professional politician - in the same way that we might look at the language of the medical or legal profession.

Looking at the language of politics as an occupation is important because it helps us to understand how language is used by those who wish to gain power, those who wish to exercise power and those who wish to keep power.

Where do they stand?

Politics/politician/political/politicise

Few words in English carry such negative connotations as the word 'politician'. **Connotation** refers to the level of meaning based on associations we attach to words, whereas **denotation** is the referential meaning, the barest core of a word's meaning. A denotative definition of the word 'politician' might be something like 'a person who is practically engaged in running a country, district or town' but the connotations surrounding the word 'politician' are nearly always negative, often strongly so.

Brewer's Dictionary of Politics, as might be expected of a dictionary on a single topic, has a very long entry for the word 'politician'. It begins with the following:

> politician : A practitioner of the art of politics, essential to the working of human society but frequently despised by those outside the political arena; indeed the word is sometimes a term of abuse.

Brewer's Dictionary is dedicated solely to words from the field of professional politics, and is aimed at readers who are likely to be interested in the subject, so there are a number of words here which attempt to give a positive gloss to the word politician. A 'practitioner' of something carries connotations of professionalism - doctors are in practice. Describing politics as an 'art', which is 'essential', also places the politician in a good light, doing work which is skilful, creative and necessary for the good of 'society', for the good of us all. Even this dictionary, though, has to concede that politicians are frequently despised, although the qualification that the despisers come from 'outside the political arena' suggests that they are not really qualified to talk – that only politicians really know the truth about what they do.

This suggestion that politicians are somehow sinister, devious figures goes back a long way. Hotspur in Shakespeare's *Henry IV Part 1* says of his opponent Bolingbroke:

> I am whipt and scourg'd with rods
> Nettled, and stung with pismires [ants], when I hear
> Of this vile politician.

while King Lear says to the blinded Gloucester:

> Get thee glass eyes
> And like a scurvy politician, seem
> To see the things thou dost not.

Because the word 'politician' carries such negative connotations, another word is required for those few politicians who achieve, and sustain almost universal popularity. If the word politician carries such a stigma, then what can we call figures such as Mahatma Gandhi, Martin Luther King or Nelson Mandela whose reputations are largely untainted with the usual connotations of deviousness? One word often used to describe them is 'statesman', a word which carries connotations of wisdom, vision, dignity – and also maleness (although even this word has undergone change in its meaning: in the early nineteenth century it carried connotations of cunning).

The French President Georges Pompidou summarised in the 1960s the different connotations of the words 'politician' and 'statesman'. He said (reflecting the assumption at the time that only men gained high office) 'A statesman is a politician who places himself at the head of the nation. A politician is a statesman who places the nation at his service.'

The noun 'politician' belongs to a family of words: 'politic', 'politics', 'political', 'politicise' are some others. The root form 'politic' comes originally from classical Greek, meaning 'city', 'citizen', 'civic', but even Greek philosophers like Plato described politics as 'nothing but corruption'. The original sense of the word, of being concerned with people and the lives they lead in organised communities, was reflected by George Orwell who said in his essay *Politics and the English Language*

(1946) 'All issues are political issues.' He too, however, viewed politics negatively, for he continued by saying 'and politics itself is a mass of lies, evasions, folly, hatred and schizophrenia'.

The idea that politics refers broadly to people and the lives they lead in organised communities rather than more narrowly to the battleground of conventional party politics became especially prominent in the 1960s. Feminists, for instance, talked of sexual politics; in using this term they were arguing that culture and ways of behaviour, including how we use language, have to be examined and changed. In this sense, then, to politicise an issue is a positive move - it is to subject it to rigorous and careful analysis and to act upon the subsequent findings. Politics, to feminists, involves far more than electing a government or voting for representatives; it involves a complete and thorough analysis of the way gender issues work in society. This was expressed at the time in the slogans 'the personal is political' and 'the political is personal'.

To describe an issue as 'political', in this usage of the word, is to demand a serious analysis and recognise the need for change; those who seek such analysis and change will often urge those close to the issue to become 'politicised'. To talk of the politics of food production, for example, suggests that there is something wrong with the way food is currently produced, something wrong with the systems which support that production, and that changes must be made. The politics of sport includes analysis of the changing social and economic structure of professional sport.

Eventually the distinctions between the use of the words 'politics/political/politicise' described here and the narrower sense of politics as the process of government can become blurred - if pressure groups seeking to politicise an issue are successful in raising awareness, then professional politicians are often quick to add the issue to their own lists of concerns.

Left, right and centre

Politics, like all spheres of social activity, has its own **code**, a term used by linguists to refer to a language variety particular to a specific group. Later in this book there will be detailed analysis of some of the linguistic rituals, involving vocabulary, grammar and discourse, which are significant features of various political activities. This introductory chapter, however, will begin by looking at some of the most common political terms and metaphors which are used by both politicians and commentators.

Key words to describe, in simple terms, the political alignment of individuals or their parties are 'left', 'right' and 'centre'. These words originate in a metonymic use, from French politics just before the French Revolution. (For a further discussion of metonymy, see Unit 2.) In the Estates-General, those who supported the King's policies sat on the right, while his opponents sat on the left. Thereafter the word 'left' has come to refer to socialist or radical groups, the word 'right' to conservative and nationalist groups. Once these words gained currency, a term was therefore needed for those who were somewhere between the two groups in their politics – these politicians were said to belong to the 'centre'.

Politics is rarely as simple as groups of three, however, and there have been many gradations of left, right and centre used in an attempt to place political friends and opponents. Those with strong views to the left or right, for example, are known as 'left/right-wingers', 'wingers' coming originally from battle (those on the edge) and more recently from sport. Those who hold less radical views are sometimes called 'left-of-centre' or 'right-of-centre'. Where your politics are positioned, however, is not as simple as it may appear, because there is no absolute, objective measure of where on the political scale, from left to right (or right to left), your ideas and opinions place you.

Instead there are terms that you might use about yourself, with positive connotations as you see them, and terms that might be used about your position, that may be less positive. The same description can carry different connotations, depending on the views of who uses them and who receives them: politicians may be pleased to call themselves 'left-wingers', whereas their opponents may use the same term critically; equally, to be in the centre may be seen positively or negatively.

One of the problems with using these terms of political positioning is that it is very hard to find a vocabulary that describes them neutrally, without connotations, whether positive or negative. How do you describe the views of those on the wings of politics? To call a view 'extreme' carries critical connotations; to call a view 'strong' does not necessarily place someone on one of the political wings – those in the centre will claim that their views are 'moderate' when judged on the left/right scale, but are 'strong' in terms of the conviction with which they are held. The word 'radical' can be equally troublesome: in the sense of getting to the root of something, it too can be applied to/claimed by politicians of all persuasions.

It seems, then, that all the terms that are used in an attempt to place politicians and their views into categories carry connotations, and that these connotations differ depending on who is using them. Some politicians are proud to be seen as having views that place them on the wing of their party. The same politicians, however, may criticise an opponent for being on the opposite wing, this time using the term with negative connotations.

As political groupings emerge, so new words are used to describe them. In the 1980s the Conservative Party ruled Britain with a large majority, and this led, as it often does, to division within its ranks. Those in the party who did not support Mrs Thatcher were called 'wets' by their opponents, a term of abuse used in public schools for those who lack courage. Adapting the metaphor, her supporters were proud to call themselves 'dry'. In time, though, the wets became more than happy with the term used to describe them and even used it themselves. This repeated a common feature of political language - terms of abuse become established and lose their negativity. The word 'Tory', originally used by English settlers in Ireland to refer to the Irish who were attacking them, was initially used as a term of abuse when applied to a group of British politicians in the eighteenth century. Eventually, though, the word became the official name of the party and is still used today, both about Conservatives and by them.

While the Conservatives were using metaphors of liquid to describe their position within the party, the Labour Party used metaphors of solidity. Radical members belonged to the 'hard left', less radical to the 'soft left'. In 1997, the Labour Party won a large majority. Its leaders had coined the term 'New Labour' to describe itself and its policies, partly to get away from the metaphor of soft/hard with its possible negative connotations. Those in the party who opposed some of the new policies called themselves 'Old Labour', hoping to construct connotations surrounding 'old' which would involve ideas of true heritage and honesty to the past, rather than being outdated or obsolete.

Where you stand - the label which you attach to yourself, or the label that is attached to you, or both - is very significant in politics. In addition to being convenient forms of quick reference for journalists and commentators, labels often say a great deal about the ideological values of those who use them. They are badges of belonging for politicians when they use them to describe themselves, but can carry either positive or negative connotations when used about them by others.

Activity

The following terms are all used as political labels. Although a number can be used as adjectives, for the sake of this activity they are all used as nouns. For each category, rearrange the order of the words so that you have a list which begins with the most negative connotations and moves to the most positive. There is no correct answer to this activity, so having come up with your own lists, if possible compare them with others to see at what points you agree/disagree and why this is so.

(a) government, regime, junta, democracy, dictatorship, faction, one-man rule – used as nouns to describe forms of government
(b) revolutionary, fundamentalist, dissident, zealot, critic, partisan, militant, separatist, paramilitary, protester, liberator – used as nouns to describe opponents of those in power
(c) militant, hawk, dove, extremist, radical, moderate – used as nouns to describe strength of attitude to a political issue

Another type of political label is that which is attached to a specific political figure. These can begin life as satirical jibes, but then shift in connotation and be seen as complimentary. When Margaret Thatcher was first referred to as 'The Iron Lady' she was being depicted as narrow and inflexible, but the term became approving when it was seen to represent qualities of toughness and resolve. Sometimes too a particular policy or policies are given a label, named after the politician deemed to be most responsible for its development: examples include 'Reagan-omics', 'Thatcherite', 'Blairite'.

Activity

1 Research as many terms as possible for the various groupings in Northern Ireland – see in particular what they call themselves and what their opponents call them.
2 By using a recently published dictionary, which will be found in most libraries, find definitions for the following political labels: Reagan-omics, Thatcherite, Blairite.
3 Political labels come and go as politicians experience their often fleeting moments of fame. Keep a list of such labels, for policies and people, as you work with the units in this book.

Satire: leaping and creeping

At the start of this unit, we saw how politicians are often seen in a negative light. We then looked at how politicians describe themselves and each other, and how political commentators, who are engaged in detailed analysis, attempt to place politicians and their views. The final part of this unit looks at how politics and politicians are presented through the means of satire.

Satire has been defined in various and often complex ways, but essentially satire involves the ridicule of either (a) individual politicians, or (b) political parties/institutions/nations, **or** in extreme cases (c) the whole human race. Whereas humour evokes laughter as an end in itself, satire aims to use laughter as a weapon, pointing out folly and by implication suggesting that political behaviour should change. There are many examples of satire which offer language students opportunities for research: in written form these range from classical literary works, such as *Gulliver's Travels* and the poems of Pope, to contemporary writings in satirical magazines. Meanwhile in the contemporary media and on stage there are many satirical works, ranging from full-blown plays through stand-up comics to quiz shows.

Whatever form or forms of satire you choose to explore, it is important as linguists to ensure that you look not only at what or who is being attacked, but also at how the satire works through its use of language and form.

Jonathan Swift's *Gulliver's Travels* was first published in 1726. As with many satirical works, on one level it depends upon **parody** for its effect. Parody is imitation of the language used by a particular writer or within a certain genre. At the time Swift wrote his book, travel writing was a popular genre, with travellers describing their adventures in ever more exotic and undiscovered locations. Using the naïve and un-sophisticated Gulliver as his narrator, Swift sends him to increasingly bizarre territories, beginning with the little people of Lilliput and end-ing with the country of the Houyhnhnms, a land ruled by horses.

Satire places the reader in a particularly crucial position. Not only must they recognise features of the genre being parodied, but they must also 'translate' the ideas from the parody to a different and more significant meaning. They can only do this translating, though, if they have the knowledge which lets them make the connection with what the writer is really referring to. So when Gulliver tells us that in Lilliput important men are given rewards for 'leaping and creeping' over or under a stick held by the King, we the readers have to work out that Swift is attacking the way power and honours are given not to the cleverest, but to those who are most adept at flattery. The key word 'creeping', with its obvious double-meaning, alerts us to this fact. In addition, most contemporary readers of Swift would have known that at that time such honours were particularly numerous.

Activity

On his first voyage, Gulliver visits Lilliput, where the inhabitants are only six inches high. As Gulliver describes the political systems of these tiny creatures, it soon becomes clear that Swift is in fact describing the political systems of England at that time. Blefuscu, the neighbouring island constantly at war with Lilliput, thus represents France.

Read the following (edited) extract from Chapter 4 of *A Voyage to Lilliput*, and then discuss the following questions.

1   The Tramecksan and Slamecksan represent the Tories (or High Church party) and the Whigs (Low Church party), the two political parties of the time in England. Why is the idea of size important to the satirical effect?

2   What satirical points about political parties are made by Swift, and how does he make them?

3   The controversy over the breaking of eggs represents the conflict between Catholic and Protestant churches in England over the previous two hundred years. What satirical points about religious divisions is Swift making, and how does he make them?

Text : Gulliver's Travels

One morning, about a fortnight after I had obtained my liberty, Reldresal, Principal Secretary (as they style him) of Private Affairs, came to my house ... I offered to lie down, that he might more conveniently reach my ear; but he chose rather to let me hold him in my hand during our conversation. He began ...

'... for above seventy moons past, there have been two struggling parties in this Empire, under the names of *Tramecksan* and *Slamecksan*, from the high and low heels on their shoes, by which they distinguish themselves ... The animosities between these two parties run so high, that they will neither eat nor drink, nor talk with each other. We compute the *Tramecksan,* or High-Heels, to exceed us in number; but the power is wholly on our side. We apprehend his Imperial Highness, the heir to the Crown, to have some tendency towards the High-Heels; at least we can plainly discover one of his heels higher than the other which gives him a hobble in his gait.

... Our histories of six thousand moons make no mention of any other regions, than the two great Empires of Lilliput and Blefuscu. Which two mighty powers have, as I was going to tell you, been engaged in a most obstinate war for six and thirty moons past. It began upon the following occasion. It is allowed on all hands, that the primitive way of breaking eggs before we eat them, was upon the the larger end: but his present Majesty's grandfather, while he was a boy, going to eat an egg, and breaking it according to the ancient practice, happened to cut one of his fingers. Whereupon the Emperor his father published an edict, commanding all his subjects, upon great penalties, to break the smaller end of their eggs. The people so highly resented this law, that our Histories tell us there have been six rebellions raised on that account; wherein one Emperor lost his life, and another his crown.

... It is computed that eleven thousand persons have, at several times, suffered death, rather than submit to break their eggs at the smaller end. Many hundred large volumes have been published upon this controversy: but the books of the Big-Endians have been long forbidden, and the whole party rendered incapable by law of holding employments. During the course of these troubles, the Emperors of Blefuscu did frequently expostulate by their ambassadors, accusing us of making a schism in religion, by offending against a fundamental doctrine of our great prophet Lustrog, in the fifty-fourth chapter of the Brundecral (which is their Alcoran). This, however, is thought to be a mere strain upon the text: for the words are these; That all true believers shall break their eggs at the convenient end.'

Commentary

The description of Gulliver holding Reldresal in his hand reminds the reader that on one level we are reading about tiny, insignificant creatures. The satire in part works because we the readers realise that these tiny people, with their fanciful titles and their petty factions, are in fact representations of the way our political systems in the big world are organised. So if these people are tiny and petty in their political affairs, then so are we. Reldresal talks with the utmost seriousness, finding nothing strange in what he says, and this effect is heightened by the way that Gulliver too accepts all this without comment. The essentially flat narrative leads the reader to work at the real significance of what is written.

The idea of size continues to be important when Swift uses high and low heels as the way the parties distinguish themselves. In their eyes, they are big differences, but in our eyes we would hardly recognise there was any difference at all, as the Lilliputians are only six inches tall. At the same time, though, we know that the Lilliputians are the same as us, so our political party differences have to be seen as just as trivial. Although Swift was writing about Tories and Whigs in the 1720s, the satire still works now.

Reldresal pompously talks of being in the more powerful party, despite this party being less numerous – Swift could be implying some sort of corruption here. Meanwhile the heir to the throne clearly wants to have it both ways; despite what Reldresal claims, the reader is aware that the heir is keeping in with both parties while at the same time to us he is appearing ridiculous.

Just as the idea of the size of a heel is ridiculously trivial, so is the issue of which end you break on a boiled egg, especially when the egg will be so tiny to our eyes. In this section it is possible to make a direct translation between the satirical picture presented by Swift (via Reldresal talking to Gulliver) and actual historical events, although the satire is just as effective without doing this. So 'his present majesty's grandfather's' accident with an egg can be translated into Henry VIII's falling out with the Catholic Church and the rise of Protestantism in Britain. What follows is a history of death, censorship, discrimination and war.

The real point of this extract, though, comes at the end. While still using Reldresal as the narrator, talking to Gulliver, Swift places in the foreground his own interpretation of what the Brundecral (or Bible) really says. Despite being a Protestant clergyman himself, Swift makes it clear that religious faith is possible without schism, and that believers should be able to get on and worship as they wish: 'all true believers shall break their eggs at the convenient end.' The word 'true' is especially important here, although on first reading its significance may be missed. 'True believers' are not those who rush to fight other sects, but those who allow religious toleration and accept that others may legitimately hold different views.

It has sometimes been said that although satire amuses, it changes nothing. Swift's clever attack on political factions and religious strife remains relevant today, which suggests that while the satire remains potent, so do the vices that it attacks.

St Albion

The magazine *Private Eye* has for many years published a regular fortnightly feature which satirises the British Prime Minister of the time. One of the best known of these features was the *Dear Bill* series in which fictional letters were written by Margaret Thatcher's husband Denis to his golfing friend. Through these letters Thatcher was presented as a strong, often tyrannical figure, married to a man who had little time for politics or politicians.

When Labour won the general election in 1997, *Private Eye* chose to present Tony Blair as the vicar of a parish called St Albion (Albion is a word sometimes used instead of Britain). Each fortnight, the vicar publishes a parish newsletter, which refers satirically to political events that have recently taken place.

Activity

In the text printed overleaf, the Rev. Blair writes about the Third Way. The real Tony Blair had just announced that 'The Third Way stands for a modernised social democracy, passionate in its commitment to social justice, but flexible, innovative and forward-looking in the means to achieve it.'

Read the text carefully and then discuss the following questions:

1   What features of parody can you detect here?
2   Unlike the extract from *Gulliver's Travels*, this text specifically satirises an individual politician. From reading this text, what satirical picture of Tony Blair emerges? What linguistic evidence have you used to deduce this?

Text: St Albion Parish News

ST ALBION PARISH NEWS

Incumbent: Rev. A.R.P. Blair MA (Oxon)

Hi, there!

As you can imagine, I've had a huge postbag this week, with all of you asking me the same question: "Vicar, what is the Third Way?"

Well, let me begin by telling you what it isn't!

The Third Way isn't just some mishy-mashy compromise, neither one thing nor the other!

Nor is it just some slick slogan dreamt up by advertising men to pull the wool over people's eyes!

No, it is something which goes right to the heart of everything that our new St Albion's is about!

What it isn't is just some half-way house, a fudge between two difficult choices!

In the old, traditional way of looking at things, there were only two paths in life.

One was the steep and stony path leading up to righteousness.

The other was the broad and easy road going down to "hell", as it used to be called!

But now I think we can all see that there is a third alternative, one that gets the best of both worlds!

The point about the Third Way, as I call it, is that it is steep, but not too steep; broad but not too broad; one that neither goes up nor down, but runs level, in a sensible, realistic, modern way!

The fact of the matter is that this is what most people these days are looking for, and it is what we at the new St Albion's are going to give them!

So, join me, as we travel along life's Third Way! And why not pop in on Sunday to sing along with the new chorus that I shall be accompanying on my guitar!

> *"There's a third way dawning,*
> *Yes, a third way dawning.*
> *There's a third way dawning*
> *And it's coming in the morning!"*

While I am on the subject of the Third Way, let me just show you how it works in practice from one or two recent examples in my own life!

There was the silly squabble between two neighbours, Mr Netanyahu and Mr Arafat, who were both claiming to own the same allotment.

This had been going on for years. I couldn't watch it happen any longer, so I called them both into the vicarage and said, "Look! Why can't you two just get it sorted, like Mr Adams and Mr Trimble have done? Why don't you just shake hands and make it up?"

Local artist Brian Bagnell brings the Third Way to life. Thanks, Brian! T.B

Both of them wanted it their way. But I showed them that there was a third way, which would have solved all their problems!

Never mind that, as soon as my back was turned, Mr Netanyahu set fire to Mr Arafat's potting shed.

At least I had showed them the way — the third way!

Similarly, when I was leading the parish ecumenical European outreach team, there was a very nasty disagreement over who should be our treasurer.

The French clergyman, Cardinal Chirac, was determined to have his own way about this. Everyone else wanted our Dutch friend, Pastor Duisenberg, to have the job.

So I showed them that there was a third way! They could both have the job on a time-sharing basis, with the Frenchman having it most of the time!

When we were all having coffee afterwards, everyone came up to thank me for doing a super job. As they all said, "We can't believe what you did in there, vicar. We won't forget this in a hurry!"

And what about those "fat cats" we hear so much about nowadays?

Once again, there are two old-fashioned views about this. One is that some local businessmen are too rich and are exploiting the poor people in our community.

The other is that, without these rich people, there would be no jobs and everybody would be poor.

But isn't the truth somewhere in-between? It usually is. It's that third way again!

So what better opportunity for me to give a big welcome to the newest member of our St Albion's team, Mr Sainsbury, who has stepped down from his old job running the supermarket in the High Street, to devote his time to helping the group-ministry here in all its good work.

In the stirring words of that much-loved old hymn,

> *"There's a third way to*
> *Tipperary,*
> *There's a third way to go..."*
> (adapted T. Blair)

Yours,

Tony

Commentary

Parody requires the reader to recognise certain linguistic and structural features that are found in a particular type of writing. So the satirical effect here depends in part upon the reader having some familiarity with parish newsletters, or at least the way in which the clergy tend to speak. Some of the features you may have noticed include the informal opening and closing, the direct appeal to 'you' as the constructed reader, the religious imagery ('one was the steep and stony path . . .'), the lecturing tone ('So, join me, as we travel along life's Third Way!'), the frequent use of exclamation marks to suggest a rather forced emphasis and the use of rhetorical questions ('And what about those "fat cats" we hear so much about nowadays?').

The presentation of Blair as a vicar in itself suggests that he is to be seen as sanctimonious and holier than thou. He is also depicted as being pompous: the reference to his degree from Oxford, and his acknow-ledged adaptation of the 'hymn' are two examples. In saying what the Third Way 'isn't', the 'real' author of the text gives clues as to how we should really see this new policy. If the fictional Blair says it is not 'some slick slogan dreamt up by advertising men', then we the readers are encouraged to believe that it is.

Blair is also presented as being rather dictatorial, behind the apparent populist idea of giving people what they want: 'The fact of the matter is that this is what most people these days are looking for, and it is what we at the new St Albion's are going to give them!' The reference to 'new' St Albion's deliberately echoes the the renaming of Labour as New Labour.

It was noted in the discussion of *Gulliver's Travels* that satire some-times makes reference to specific people and events. Here they are made obvious by the use of names: the Arab/Israeli conflict, the Irish situation and problems in the EEC are all referred to in a thinly veiled way. The Rev. Blair's suggestion that he helped solve problems is obviously not true ; he is depicted as ultimately ineffective, despite his self-congratulation.

Extension

There are many literary works which provide material for the analysis of politics and political systems.

Thomas More's *Utopia* (1516) is an early satirical work, which intro-duced the word 'utopian' into the English language. Originally written in Latin, it describes the political systems of an imaginary land and in the process comments on the politics of England at the time.

Many satirical novels are essentially dystopian — in other words, they depict, in an imaginative form, the worst of all worlds, and in the process highlight the writer's fears about the politics of their time. The following are useful starting points for students who are interested in research in this area:

Samuel Butler — *Erewhon*
Aldous Huxley — *Brave New World*
George Orwell — *1984* and *Animal Farm*
Anthony Burgess — *A Clockwork Orange*
Margaret Atwood — *The Handmaid's Tale*

Visual as well as verbal satire can be seen in political cartoons, which could form another potential area of research.

What do they stand for?

Aims of this unit

This unit will focus in particular on how language tells us a great deal about the **ideology** of those who use it — including politicians, and those who report on the work of politicians. It will focus in particular on metaphor, metonymy, analogy and transitivity, all terms which will be explained as they are discussed.

The problem of truth

Politicians and other public figures often complain about bias in the media, about media 'witch-hunts': instead of reporting the truth, they claim, the media present a distorted picture which serves their own interests. The BBC is one particular focus for such complaints because it often claims to be impartial in its news reporting and concerned only with broadcasting the objective truth. Sometimes the complaints revolve around the fact that a story has been broken at all, at other times they concern the presentation of the story, including the language used. The philosopher A. J. Ayer wrote in 1936 that 'the terms true and false connote nothing, but function ... simply as marks of assertion and denial'. In other words, there is no such thing as absolute truth - what we call a truth is in fact an assertion which we ourselves believe in. By this definition truth is both relative and subjective. The whole idea of 'truth' is very problematic at the best of times, but when it relates to how a political story is reported then it is especially so.

When a television news team report a story, they make a number of decisions which will affect how the story is received by the audience. Where they position the camera, the sequence in which they show events and the language they use will all determine the overall picture we get. In making these decisions they are reflecting an ideological view; there is no such thing as an unbiased report, no such thing as 'neutral' language. To say 'The White House today threatened Saddam Hussein with military action over the UN inspectors affair' (see below) gives a perspective which essentially favours the American position. It would be just as possible to present the story from different perspectives, from different ideological standpoints.

This does not mean, though, that language is merely the tool of cynical manipulation; that because you can report the same story in different ways there are no such things as ethical or moral behaviour, that one political policy is no more fair and just than another. Language is a means of communication, a means of presenting and shaping argument and political argument is ideological, in that it comes from a series of beliefs. Language is not something somehow separate from the ideas it contains, but the way language is used says a great deal about how the ideas have been shaped. When analysing the language of a political text, therefore, it is important to look at the way the language reflects the ideological position of those who have created it, and how the ideological position of the readers will affect their response too.

Philosophers distinguish between validity and truth in argument and this is a useful distinction to make here. A valid argument is one where the logic is correct; it does not have to lead to a 'true' conclusion. Equally, a 'true' conclusion can come from an invalid argument. This means that the relationship between language and truth is more complex than is sometimes thought. When a parent tells a child to 'tell the truth', it is a relatively straightforward matter. To expect that a political journalist, or a politician, can 'tell the truth' just as easily is much more problematic, because it fails to take account of the fact that both the creator and the receiver of the text bring ideological values to it. Indeed, it could be argued that clear personal attacks on politicians are seen by the audience as just that - personal attacks. Much less likely to be seen for what they are are the news reports which claim an objectivity they cannot possibly have.

Metaphor and metonymy

Both **metaphor** and **metonymy** are frequently used in the language of politics. They are only one aspect of political discourse, but they are useful starting points for looking at some of the ways in which political language operates.

Metaphor refers to when a word or a phrase is used which establishes a comparison between one idea and another. When a politician is said to 'take flak' from an opponent, politics is being compared to warfare, with the politician metaphorically being shot at. On the other hand, it may be the politician who is 'on the offensive, targeting' his opponents by 'launching an attack' on their policies.

Metonymy involves replacing the name of something with something that is connected to it, without being the whole thing. For example, the President of the United States, his government and advisors, are sometimes replaced by the much simpler term 'The White House', which is the presidential residence and administrative centre. Similarly, when an announcement is made by a member of the British royal family, it is often described as follows: 'Buckingham Palace today denied claims that the royal family is out of touch with the people.' In other words the building where they live – Buckingham Palace – replaces the name of the people who live there – the royal family. The above announcement without use of metonymy would read 'The royal family today denied claims that they are out of touch with the people' or 'The Queen today denied . . .'

Activity

The following text is taken from an imaginary news report about a music award ceremony. It has been deliberately constructed to show examples of metaphor and metonymy. If you are confident that you understand these concepts, cover up the commentary below and see how well you can

(a)   Identify the examples of metaphor and metonymy, and
(b)   Explain the comparisons that are being made.

If you are less sure about these concepts, then read the commentary once you have read the text, and make sure that you understand the explanations.

19

Text : Music Awards

> British music triumphed when home-grown bands swept the board at the World Pop Awards. The Albert Hall was treated to a feast of celebration as many of the world's leading bands received their accolades.
>
> There was also a morsel of controversy when the Deputy Prime Minister was half-drowned by a water jug hurled by rising star Jake Thrower.

Commentary

Although some of the metaphors will have been easy to detect, others may have been less so because their metaphorical origins have become embedded in English. Goatly (1997) uses the term 'inactive' to describe metaphors which over time have become 'lexicalised' – defined in dictionaries with their new meaning. For instance, is the word 'star' used metaphorically here? Technically it is a metaphor, but we use the word so frequently to refer to famous people, that any dictionary would now include a reference to a celebrity as one definition of the word 'star'.

Metaphors are identified first. Examples of metonymy then follow:

Metaphors:

1. triumphed: literally a victory procession, but here used to suggest success.
2. home-grown: from the idea of gardening, but here meaning from this country.
3. swept the board: from a game such as chess or drafts, here meaning won everything.
4. treated to a feast: from food and eating, here meaning a large amount (and perhaps high quality).
5. leading: from the idea of being at the front of an army, a race, etc., here referring to success.
6. accolades: originally referring to being knighted with a sword, here referring to an award.
7. morsel: this relates back to the feast, this time meaning a small part.
8. half-drowned: a form of exaggeration, as really he got a bit wet.
9. rising star: light in the sky or famous person.

Metonymy:
1   British music: a convenient phrase to use as a short form for saying 'a large number of British bands'. British music cannot triumph, only individual bands can.
2   The Albert Hall: this is the venue, but it is the people inside it who are actually treated to the celebration.
3   a water jug: this is a more technical point, but it would be the water that would half-drown the Deputy Prime Minister, not the jug which contained it.

The power of metaphors

Recent work on semantics in English has investigated the place of metaphor in everyday speech (for example, Lakoff and Johnson 1980; Goatly 1997). Metaphor is deeply embedded in the way we construct the world around us and the way that world is constructed for us by others. An example of this process involves the metaphorical idea that a lesson is a journey: we take a difficult topic 'step by step'; if we cannot conclude an idea we 'go round in circles'; if we lose relevance we 'go off in the wrong direction'; if we are successful in understanding we 'arrive at a conclusion'; if we are unsuccessful we are 'lost' or 'stuck'.

Two common sources of metaphor in politics are sport and war, both of which involve physical contests of some sort. Both politicians themselves, and those who report politics, use these metaphors. Boxing metaphors are particularly common, conveying a sense of toughness and aggression, especially when an election is seen as a fight between two main protagonists who are nearly always male. When the British Election of 1997 was announced, one newspaper had the headline 'The Gloves Are Off', suggesting not just boxing, but a bare-knuckle fight.

In the USA, baseball metaphors abound in politics: 'a whole new ball game', 'a ball park figure', 'to play ball', to be 'back at first base' and 'spin' (see below). These metaphors are increasingly used in British political discourse too, but baseball's equivalent game, cricket, offers others: 'to keep your eye on the ball'; 'batting on a sticky wicket'; to be 'stumped' by or to 'play a straight bat' to a question.

When Blair's supporters in 1997 wanted to suggest that if he won, his government would act promptly on issues, they used a metaphor taken from warfare and promised to 'hit the ground running'. This phrase originates in the idea of soldiers leaping from combat helicopters and running straight into action. After Ronald Reagan's poor showing in a televised debate in 1984, his supporters promised a campaign of 'damage control'. The word 'campaign' is itself a reference to battle, and in campaigns 'political battles are won', 'leads are surrendered'.

It is worth noting that this sense of politics being seen as a sort of warfare through the use of metaphors can be seen in reverse when real war is talked about. The shadow boxing of party politics, with its metaphors of battle, becomes much less gung-ho when real victims in real wars are to be explained away. In the 1990s dead civilians became 'collateral damage' in a form of political language which wanted to hide the horror, while the mass evacuation (and often murder) of civilians belonging to the other side became 'ethnic cleansing'.

Gibbs (1994) points out that metaphors from sport and war are 'not just rhetorical devices for talking about politics, for they exemplify how people ordinarily conceive of politics ... for instance metaphors from sports and war often delude people into believing that negotiation and compromise are forbidden by the rules.' In other words, because so much language which surrounds political issues is rooted in metaphors of war, contest or sport – even if we are not always consciously aware of these roots – then we have no idea that politics can be anything other than confrontational, that it could in fact involve agreement and consensus. The key metaphors of politics involve concepts of enemies and opponents, winners and losers; they do not suggest that government could be achieved through discussion, co-operation, working together.

Activity

The text opposite is from a leaflet sent to voters in one British constituency during the election of 1997. The Referendum Party stood for one issue – that the British electors should have the chance to vote in a referendum on whether Britain should leave the European Commission, an organisation with its headquarters in Brussels.

1   Look closely at the metaphorical language used in this extract. Look first at examples of metonymy. Then find the metaphorical references to war and say what they contribute to the persuasive power of the text.

2   What other linguistic methods are used in an attempt to persuade the reader? Look for instance at the way pronouns are used, i.e. 'you', 'we', etc. Consider also the way graphological features such as highlighting parts of the text are used.

3   How are the paragraphs connected to each other so that a cohesive argument is formed?

Text : Referendum Party

Your last chance to vote for a referendum on who should run Britain – Westminster or Brussels.

This General Election is by far the most important in Britain's history. It will decide whether our country finally surrenders her independence to Brussels and we become a mere province of Europe.

Already, we have seen our fishing industry destroyed and our businesses swamped with regulations from the army of unelected bureaucrats in Brussels.

And already, laws made by the European Commission are the laws of this land and take precedence over our own.

What's more, our economy must now be run for the benefit of the whole of Europe. The Government has surrendered the right to put us first when it comes to creating jobs and security for our future.

And if the Eurocrats have their way, we will soon be forced to abandon our 3 remaining rights – to decide foreign policy, to organise our own national security and control our own borders.

With these rights gone, Britain will be little more than a province in a new country called Europe. That is why this General Election is so crucial.

The politicians have put off discussion of further integration until after the Election. But there's no doubt what they intend.

It was the Conservatives who signed the treaties that surrendered our independence. And, as we all know, Labour are committed to Europe.

We believe the politicians have no right to surrender our national independence without a proper referendum.

We have been deceived for far too long. Most people thought they were voting for a common trading market in 1975. How wrong they were.

And now, when we realise the truth, we are being denied the democratic right to decide our future.

This is an issue which towers above party politics. That's why, on this one occasion, we ask you to lay aside your traditional party loyalty and support the Referendum Party.

In this constituency, and over 550 others around Britain, people will be standing as Referendum Party Candidates.

None is a politician, nor wishes to become one. But all care passionately that the British people should make their views on Europe heard through a referendum.

Every single vote for the Referendum Party will count. The total number of votes cast for the Party across the country will send a clear message to the politicians that the people want a referendum.

And any Referendum Party candidates elected to Parliament will fight vigorously for the interests of their constituents.

When a full referendum has been achieved, the Party will disband. Then you can vote once again for your usual party.

But now, just once, we urge you to put your country before your party.

Printed by Banks Hoggins O'Shea, 54 Baker Street, London W1M 1DJ on behalf of the publisher: The Referendum Party, 1st Floor, Dean Bradley House, 52 Horseferry Road, London SW1P 2AF.

Commentary

Both the headline and the picture at the start of this leaflet use metonymy. Two place names are used to represent two parliaments – the London district of 'Westminster' for the British parliament and 'Brussels' for the European parliament. Brussels, as representation of the European parliament, is repeated in the picture. A sign hangs from the door of number 10 saying that the occupants have left and moved to Brussels. What this actually signifies is that, according to the Referendum Party, the British government (represented by 'Number 10') has given up its power by handing it over to the European parliament in Brussels. This picture therefore sums up, in symbolic form, the content of the whole message which follows.

There are many metaphorical references to war: the Referendum Party is fighting a last-ditch battle to keep Britain free of external influence; 'our' fishing industry has been 'destroyed', 'our' businesses 'swamped' by an 'army' of bureaucrats. 'Our' government has already 'surrendered' too much – this word is used three times – but the party will 'fight vigorously' on 'our' behalf. All this suggests that this is an argument about a desperate battle to survive, that many valued ways of life have been lost and that this is the very last chance to save ourselves.

Pronoun reference is always important in putting over a piece of political persuasion. The very first word 'your' gives an immediate sense that the reader is being addressed personally, although there is also a sense that 'you' is not just the single reader but also everyone in the country. Politicians often wish to suggest that even though they are trying to persuade us to a point of view, we already agree with them; thus the pronoun 'we' appears in the first paragraph and at numerous other points too. 'We' gives a sense of collectivity, of us all being in this together, so 'we have been deceived' in the past, but no longer. Later in the extract 'we' becomes the Referendum Party urging us to vote for them, as in 'we ask you to lay aside your traditional party loyalty'.

Contrast of comparison in adjectives and adverbials is called **degree**. Political parties like to stress the importance of their views, so not surprisingly a **superlative** form appears at once: this general election is 'by far the most important' in Britain's history. This sense of degree is repeated later when the election is called 'so crucial'. Verbs and **adverbials** are also very strong in their meaning: this is an issue which metaphorically 'towers' above party politics and we all 'care passionately' about having our views heard.

As stated above, the picture gives, in metonymic form, the gist of the argument – that Britain has given in to Europe. Nonetheless the text needs to expand upon this and make it absolutely clear. Each paragraph has either one or two sentences and is carefully placed so that an argument is built up, leading to the inevitability of the final message — vote for the Referendum Party. The way a text develops and holds together is called **cohesion**. Cohesion in this extract is achieved, in particular, by the way many paragraphs open with clear connections to what has gone before. The word 'and' opens four paragraphs, suggesting an argument being continued, with 'what's more' doing a similar job. In one case 'already' which opens paragraph two, is followed by 'and already' in paragraph three. 'With these rights' and 'this is an issue' show **anaphoric** demonstrative reference. The deictic words 'these' and 'this' act as anaphoric pointers. In other words, they point back to something that has already been mentioned. Cohesion is also maintained by the **graphological** device of bold type — every so often a step in the argument is signalled by the use of bold type. Inevitably the summation of the argument, the call to vote, is in bold print, and begins with the words 'but now' which indicate that something different has to happen this time because 'we have been deceived for far too long'.

Two other points worth noting are that although this is a political leaflet calling on people to vote in an election, the word 'politician' is, as seen in Unit 1, used as a term of abuse. None of this party's candidates 'is a politician, nor wishes to become one'. And the final call to vote, placing your country first, not only appeals to a sense of nationalism, but also echoes the famous World War One poster saying 'your country needs you'.

There are other areas that you may have noticed in your answers — the references to the other parties (but never in the bold print sections), the fact that deceitful opponents are 'wrong' but that 'we realise the truth', the 'we' referring not only to them, but to us the readers too. All of these contribute to a text whose major purpose is to persuade the reader to do just one thing — vote for the Referendum Party.

The power of metonymy

Earlier in this unit, the following was used as an example of metonymy: (a) 'Buckingham Palace today denied claims that the royal family is out of touch with the people' and the following was given as an alternative version without metonymy: (b) 'The royal family today denied claims that they are out of touch with the people.' It might, at first glance, seem as though there is not much difference between the two statements, but on closer investigation the meaning is not the same. In (a), the royal family, who are at the centre of the claims, do not themselves seem to speak. Indeed the speaking is done for them by a building which will be, in many minds, a large and impressive structure. In (b), though, they have to speak for themselves - it is they personally who have to deny what has been said about them. It can be argued that (a), therefore, gives a more sympathetic picture of the royal family than (b).

Lakoff and Johnson (1980) give as an example of metonymy the phrases 'she's just a pretty face', 'there are a lot of faces out there in the audience', and 'we need some new faces around here'. Here the face as part of the human body stands for or represents the whole human body – this idea of part for whole is also sometimes referred to as **synecdoche.** Lakoff and Johnson go on to show that metonymic uses are not random, but systematic, in that they show how we organise our thoughts, actions and attitudes. An example of how this works can be seen in the way we use 'face' to represent the whole person. If you ask to look at a photo of someone, and are shown a facial portrait, then you will almost certainly be satisfied that you have seen the person. If, however, you are shown a picture of their legs, without the face, you would demand to see more. In other words in our culture we get our basic information about people from their faces, rather than their bodies.

Metonymy, then, involves replacing the name of something with something that is connected to it, without being the whole thing itself; and in doing so it affects the audience's perception of and attitude to the original thing. An example quoted at the beginning of this unit comes from a BBC news broadcast concerning growing tension between the USA and Iraq: 'The White House today threatened Saddam Hussein with military action over the UN inspectors affair.' The metonymy is where 'the White House' replaces 'the president and his advisers' and 'Saddam Hussein' replaces 'the country/people of Iraq'.

In this example the journalist writing the report has used metonymy in a way which gives a very favourable view of the American position. There is a distinct advantage for the president in not himself being named. Attacking a foreign country is dangerous, not something an individual would want to be held responsible for - it is much better if the threat is reported as emerging from an impressive building which contains a suitably impressive collection of top people. On the other hand, by using Saddam Hussein to represent the country he ruled, it appears that he alone would suffer the results of the attack - innocent bystanders are not involved. When the news is more cheerful, however, involving success of some sort, then the president will be more than happy to be named in full. So when the USA contributed to peace talks in Ireland, the BBC reported: 'President Clinton was urged by all sides to continue his efforts on behalf of peace in Ireland.'

The British equivalent for the White House is 'Number 10', standing for 10 Downing Street, which is the official residence of the Prime Minister. Hence 'Number 10 today announced further changes to the Social Security system' or 'Number 10 today denied a split in party ranks.'

No building has contributed as much to the language of politics as the Watergate building in Washington. In 1972 the building, which housed the Democratic Party, was broken into by supporters of the Republican president Richard Nixon. This led to a major political crisis in the USA, culminating in the resignation and disgrace of the president. The whole long, drawn-out process became known as the Watergate scandal, the building's name conveniently standing in place of detailed descriptions of very complex procedures.

Since then, however, the suffix 'gate' has been used with increasing frequency, and ingenuity, to describe all sorts of scandals in most English-speaking countries. Where one text uses reference to another this is known as **intertextuality**. When President Carter's brother Billy showed signs of alcoholism, it was known as 'Billygate'. When local councillors in Doncaster, Yorkshire, were accused of malpractice, the Yorkshire Post called the scandal 'Donnygate'. Scandal over the Prince of Wales' relationship with Camilla Parker Bowles was known as 'Camillagate'.

When President Clinton was accused of having affairs with four different women during his presidency, the crisis was labelled 'sexgate' or 'fornigate'. The latter worked on a number of linguistic levels: the word is a play upon the word 'fornicate', to have sex with; it contains the sound of the word 'four'; the use of 'gate' suggests scandal. Even more inter-textually complex was the headline at the same time which said 'All the President's Women.' A famous film of the Watergate scandal was called *All the President's Men.* So the link between Watergate and any scandal is taken a stage further by making a verbal play with the title of a film about the scandal.

The power of analogy

So far this unit has looked at examples of metaphor and metonymy, and how they can show the ideological positions of the users. Metaphor and metonymy operate at word or phrase level, establishing comparison between one idea and another. Sometimes, though, political argument involves comparison on a larger scale – this is known as **analogy**, and analogy shows ideological positions too. Analogy operates by comparing two objects of different types; but these two objects have certain elements in common. Objects of the first kind have a certain characteristic;

it is not known if objects of the second kind have it or not, but by analogy we conclude that since objects of the two kinds have certain things in common, they may have other things in common as well.

This may sound rather complicated, but in fact analogy is used frequently. In order to understand human behaviour, say aggression for example, researchers sometimes study animal behaviour in the wild - because monkeys react to stress in a certain way, this tells us something about human behaviour too, they argue.

This can be schematised as follows:

◎ Objects of type *x* (i.e. monkeys) have certain properties (live in communities, sometimes fight)
◎ Objects of type *y* (i.e. humans) have similar properties (live in communities, sometimes fight)
◎ Objects of type *x* show stress under certain conditions
◎ Therefore objects of type *y* show stress under the same conditions.

The 'strength' of an analogy depends very much on the degree of similarity between the objects being compared and whether they are similar in ways that are relevant to the argument being made. In the example above, some scientists would claim that humans and monkeys have lots in common and so, by analogy, how monkeys behave says a lot about human behaviour. Others would say, though, that human society is very different from primate society, so any comparison between the two is impossible.

A favourite economic argument put forward by Margaret Thatcher used analogy: comparing the economy of the nation with the economy of an individual household, she said that just as it was dangerous for a family to run up a debt, so it was dangerous for a country to do the same. Therefore the government had to spend less than it might ideally want to. In the sense that it appealed to what people could readily understand - their own finances - it was a highly effective comparison. Many expert economists, though, said that economics on a national scale bear little resemblance to those on a personal level, and so her analogy was a false one. Her use of the family budget and a fear of debt as points of comparison showed that ideologically she held certain views about the typical family and its values.

Commenting on a political scandal, a journalist wrote: 'Wherever you have power you will have sleaze. It's like a dog and fleas.'

The problem with this analogy is that there is no likeness between holding power and being a dog, however witty the analogy may sound. When analogies are used, therefore, the reader must not just accept them but must evaluate their strength as a piece of argument.

The following question was put by a broadcaster to an Irish Protestant politician who was objecting to the fact that he was not allowed to parade through a Catholic residential area.

> What are you making so much fuss about? I'm not allowed to enter Buckingham Palace and I don't complain.

Analyse the component parts of this analogy and say whether you think the analogy is weak or strong.

The art of spin

With ever increasing media coverage of politics, and competition among the media to give the most sensationalist portrayals of political events, political parties have increasingly used public relations experts to channel facts to the media, and to put the best possible construction on events. In the 1980s in America, these PR experts were labelled 'spin-doctors' by media commentators. The word 'spin' relates to baseball, putting spin on the ball being a pitcher's technique in an attempt to fool or deceive an opponent. The word 'doctor' suggests a healer, someone who resolves a crisis (although as a verb it can also mean to cheat as in to doctor someone's drink). Thus a 'spin-doctor' is someone who deceives, who presents a false picture to suit the politician – once again the activities of politicians are seen to be devious. It should also be noted that politicians do not admit to employing 'spin-doctors' themselves; they would refer to their press agent, or some such similar term. Nonetheless, they regularly complain about spin-doctoring when it is their political opponents who are putting out messages.

How the spin is placed on a story will depend upon a number of things. These include: the overall political effect that is desired, either celebrating success or ridiculing failure; the way information is presented; and what metaphorical uses are brought in to influence the audience's view of events. When OFSTED (the Office of Standards in Education in England) conducted research in 1997 into how well literacy was taught in London schools, they found that 66 per cent of lessons were satisfactory, and 33 per cent unsatisfactory. Their spin-doctors presented these findings by focusing on the fact that one in three lessons was inadequate. This led to headlines such as 'Teachers fail pupils' and 'Reading standards plummet as inspectors find catalogue of failure.' An alternative spin could have been put on the story, however, if the figures had been approached differently. If the main focus of the story had been on the two out of three lessons which succeeded, it might have led to headlines such as 'Teachers raise literacy standards', or 'Literacy standards rise.'

As can be seen in the examples quoted above, spin often involves either claiming credit or distributing blame. One way of exploring how blame or credit are attributed is to look at the way **transitivity** works in a text. Transitivity involves looking at the language used to describe:

- what happens
- who the participants are (both those who do something and those affected by what is done)
- what the circumstances are.

Blame or credit can be attributed, for instance, by either emphasising the role of a participant or by minimising it. This process can include the naming labels given to the participant as well as the grammatical fore-grounding or backgrounding of their role. (Another helpful metaphor to describe this process is to talk of weight: at what points in a clause or sentence is the most weight applied?) One of the most obvious ways in which participants can be foregrounded, backgrounded or omitted entirely is by using either the **active** or **passive voice**. In simple terms this can be shown as follows:

> Chancellor announces tax cuts (active voice - Chancellor given prominence)

> Tax cuts announced by Chancellor (passive voice - less prominence given to Chancellor)

> Tax cuts announced (passive voice, actor deleted - no reference to Chancellor at all)

Newspaper headlines are useful starting points for looking at how trans-itivity works. In July 1998 the British Chancellor of the Exchequer, Gordon Brown, announced substantial funding for health and education - far more money than political pundits had forecast. As far as headlines for this story went, there were essentially three possible ingredients:

- more money was made available for public services
- Gordon Brown, the Chancellor of the Exchequer, made the announcement in Parliament

◎   health and education were the two services awarded most of the extra money.

Which of these elements was given most weight, which was given least or even none at all, and the metaphorical associations raised by the choice of vocabulary give some clues as to the ideological/political position of the newspaper.

BROWN GOES FOR BROKE IN 57BN SPENDING SPREE
(*Daily Telegraph*)

The Chancellor is here given a very formal naming label, his surname only. The main clause in the headline is 'Brown goes for broke'; this is given most weight with a subject (Brown) who is actively doing something (goes for broke). The word 'broke' is a deliberate pun, because to 'go for broke' means risking everything, and to be 'broke' is to be without money. The amount of money is quoted, but it is additionally described as a 'spending spree', carrying connotations of profligacy, or carelessness. What the money is to be spent on is not mentioned at all; most people would support spending on health and education, but as they are not mentioned it is the ideas of going broke and of over-spending which are most emphasised. This analysis suggests that the *Daily Telegraph* is not a supporter of the Labour Party.

40BN AID FOR NHS/SCHOOLS (*Newcastle Journal*)

This time the sum of money quoted is lower than in the *Daily Telegraph*. The money is 'aid' rather than a 'spree', and it is help that is being given to named good causes. So all the weight is placed upon a phrase which details the money and the recipients. The donor, though, is not named and there is no verb suggesting any action – there is an implied sense that the money has come from the government, but it has not been personalised in any way as belonging to the Chancellor. This paper appears to support the action that has been taken and can be assumed to be broadly supportive of the Labour Party.

HAND OF GORD (the *Sun*)

Understanding this headline involves an awareness of the phrase 'hand of God'. This on one level might refer to the religious idea of the hand of God being generous, giving blessings, but it also strongly echoes the claim by the footballer Maradona that it was the 'hand of God' which intervened when he infamously punched the ball into the goal during a World Cup game between England and Argentina. The punning on God/Gord, which is at the heart of the headline, may possibly carry the implication that Gordon Brown is playing at being God, but overall this seems unlikely. Gord is a shortening of Gordon, so only one of the three possible ingredients is mentioned in this phrase, the main participant; there is no direct reference to money, certainly no amount, and no mention of the good causes. It would seem here that the *Sun* is most interested in the linguistic joke made by its headline; there is no obvious support or criticism of the Labour Party here, at least as far as the headline goes. It is also worth noting that metonymy is used here, if Brown's hand is seen to stand for the Chancellor of the Exchequer being generous.

Activity

Exploring the way transitivity works, then, can help you to see how praise or blame are attributed and to understand the ideological values of the producers of texts. Following on from the examples quoted above, these headlines also appeared covering the same political story:

SPEND, SPEND, SPEND

BROWN SPLASHES OUT 40BN

GORDON OPENS HIS WALLET

HE'S JUST SPENT 56BN AND HE'S THINKING OF THE NEXT ELECTION

Analyse the language of each headline and say what spin is put on the story in each case. There is no commentary for this activity.

Extension

Opinion polls are used by the media to assess public perception on political issues. They are used frequently in the run-up to elections to see how people are likely to vote, and they are used during the lifetime of a government to see how the public views the government's performance. Using a carefully selected sample, the pollsters interview people about their views on various issues. The findings in part depend upon what questions are actually asked, and how they are phrased. The analysis of the figures often depends upon the political views of the journalist who interprets them, while the political parties interpret them in the way which makes them look most favourable. In other words, from the data provided, both journalists and politicians apply their own particular spin.

The following questions and figures are based upon a typical poll.

1   The government has been in power for a year. Would you say it has done

     a very good job   11%
     a fairly good job   38%
     a fairly bad job   26%
     a very bad job   5%
     no opinion   8%

2   Do you think the government has been honest and trustworthy, or not?

     honest and trustworthy   49%
     not honest and trustworthy   39%
     no opinion   12%

3   Do you think that public services have improved, got worse, or stayed the same since the government came to power?

     improved   12%
     got worse   16%
     stayed the same 65%

4   Do you feel confident that this government will improve standards of living during its time in office?

     yes   30%
     no   15%
     they will stay the same 50%
     no opinion   5%

There are three tasks:

1   Produce headlines on the poll for different types of newspaper. In doing this, consider the type of newspaper and its usual political position. Make sure that you include some headlines which favour the government and others that are hostile.

2   Write up the story to accompany one of your headlines, making sure that you apply a spin which clearly favours or criticises the government. No specific government has been named here, so you can apply your story to any current government and its leaders that you know about.

3   The leader of the government and then the leader of the Opposition are asked the following question: what are your reactions to the latest opinion poll on the government's performance?

Write their answers to this question.

Making speeches

Making speeches is a vital part of the politician's role in announcing policy and persuading people to agree with it. Analysing such speeches is a popular source of students' own research in this field. This unit will look at some of the most common features of political speeches and give some indication of how their linguistic methods can be analysed.

Rhetoric is defined by Cockcroft and Cockcroft in their book *Persuading People* (1992) as 'the art of persuasive discourse' using the word 'discourse', here to refer to both spoken and written communication. The Greek philosopher Aristotle (384-322 BC) wrote extensively on the 'art' of rhetoric, seeing it as an important part of human activity, and so worth categorising and defining in great detail. Plato, on the other hand, believed rhetoric to be about the manipulation of an audience by people who were essentially insincere in their motives. Neither saw rhetoric as concerned only with government, but as a factor in all human communication; the skills of rhetoric were taught in early school systems in Britain, long before subjects like English Language or Literature were invented.

Although rhetoric, in the sense that the Cockcrofts use the word, relates to all forms of human communication, the word has tended to be used much more frequently to refer to speech and even more specifically to a certain type of formal public speaking. Rhetorical skills, in the sense of persuasive public speaking, have always had emphasis in the American education system, and they are present in the British system too. Debating societies are a common feature in many schools, colleges and universities, and debating competitions are popular. The English and Welsh National Curriculum refers to formal debating as an important part of students' education in Speaking and Listening.

One of the most common features of this formal debating is that it is the *skills* of speaking persuasively that are far more important than a personally held belief in the topic under debate. In competitions, for instance, debating teams are given a proposition and are told which side they must argue. They are judged on their rhetorical skills, and their ability to speak persuasively, rather than the honesty of their views. Students when debating formally are encouraged to see insincerity as perfectly acceptable, provided the rhetorical skills are good enough. The adversarial legal systems of many countries could also be said to reward rhetorical skill rather than honesty and truth; good lawyers are often seen as those who can persuade a jury to agree with their case, rather than adjudicate on what really happened.

There are many forms of public speaking other than debating and the law, however: the college lecture; the religious sermon; the social club AGM are all examples of events where formal speeches are made. The assumption would be in all these cases that sincerely held views are expressed, but that rhetorical skills are going to be needed if the audience is to both pay attention and be persuaded.

So in some instances we place the skills of rhetoric above the value of honesty (as Plato indicated); in others we hope that the skills of rhetoric will reinforce our good intentions (as Aristotle claimed). When we come to political speeches, though, the position is less clear. No doubt the politicians themselves would argue that they wish to put forward policies that they genuinely believe in. More cynical listeners, though, might argue that the real purpose, at least for those politicians whom they see as untrustworthy, is to manipulate the audience into agreeing with policies which really serve only the desire of the politician to gain or keep power. There is no simple answer to this dilemma, because concepts like honesty and sincerity cannot be measured against any absolute standard.

This unit will focus on a few of the most common persuasive devices and the effects of modern media on the way politicians make speeches. Before doing so, though, it is helpful to refer to Aristotle's classification of the means of persuasion into three broad categories; Cockcroft and Cockcroft describe these as:

(a) persuasion through personality and stance
(b) persuasion through the arousal of emotion
(c) persuasion through reasoning.

Although this unit will focus most on the last of these three, the linguistic reasoning cannot be persuasive without the other two categories as well. All three categories will be used by the speaker as part of the performance; how well they are constructed, and how each member of the audience responds to them, will decide whether the politician is seen as sincere or manipulative.

The soundbite age

Politicians nowadays tend to make most of their public speeches to invited audiences of their own supporters - at events such as party conferences and party rallies. This was not always the case. Up to the 1960s political speeches tended to be more numerous and offer more open access to anyone who wanted to attend. This meant that most speeches were interrupted by hecklers - and the politicians' skill was often judged by how well these hecklers were put down.

These days, although the audience in the hall is vital to the whole process - as will be seen shortly - the real audiences are the millions who will either read about the speeches in newspapers or hear/see them on radio and television. The speeches are often written for the speakers, with leading politicians having teams of speech writers to prepare their material for them. Speeches are distributed in advance to the press so that they can catch the next day's newspapers and to broadcasters so that they can cover the speeches in evening news bulletins. However, the broadcasters will not, unless the circumstances are very special, transmit the whole speech, which means that the speeches must contain highlights which can be shown, in much the same way that the goals are shown from a football match, or the wickets falling in cricket. These highlights from speeches are sometimes called **soundbites** - they are carefully engineered excerpts, which the speakers hope in advance will receive attention. (The word 'soundbite' derives in part from the idea of a computer byte, which in turn comes from a bite or chunk taken out of something.) The audience in the hall, although not really the primary audience for the speech, have a vital role to play in the success of the soundbite.

Politicians are often accused of speaking claptrap, and Max Atkinson (1984) traces the origin of the word 'claptrap'. He quotes a definition of the word as meaning 'a trick, device of language designed to catch applause' and for the soundbites to work, the audience in the hall have to endorse what is being said by giving enthusiastic support. In other words they must happily fall for the claptrap.

The importance of three

Atkinson notes from his survey of speeches that one of the most common means of eliciting approval is the use of what he calls a 'list of three'. Whatever the nature of the speech act, political speech or casual conversation, the three-part list is attractive to the speaker and listener because it is embedded in certain cultures as giving a sense of unity and completeness: 'on your marks, get set, go!' is the traditional way to start a race; omit either of the first two components and the runners are unlikely to respond.

Activity

Compile a list of well-known references which either include the number three, or form lists with three parts. Consider idiomatic phrases, literary references, religious references, popular jokes, song titles, nursery rhymes, children's stories, etc.

In political speeches, the lists of three can be simple repetition, as in the chant at marches against the policy of Margaret Thatcher when she was in power:

Maggie, Maggie, Maggie
Out, Out, Out

or in Tony Blair's soundbite when he stated at the time of the 1997 general election that his main concern was:

Education, Education, Education

or Republican Henry Hyde in the aftermath of the Monica Lewinsky affair, saying that he would act according to his sense of 'duty, duty, duty'.

Abraham Lincoln in his Gettysburg Address of 1863 used a slight modification of this simple repetition by using a different preposition in front of the words 'the people' :

Government *of* the people,
By the people,
For the people.

Winston Churchill, praising the efforts of the Battle of Britain fighter pilots, said in 1940:

Never in the field of human conflict has
so much
been owed by so many
to so few.

The word 'so' is repeated three times, but there is also a contrast between 'so much/so many' and the last of the three 'so few'.

The effect of these lists does not rest solely in the repetition: they are spoken aloud, so **prosodic features**, such as pitch, tempo and rhythm, also play a major part in their effect. Remember too that non-verbal features will contribute to the effect, at least for those who can see the speaker on television or in the hall.

The three-part list does not have to be mere repetition. It can have different words, but with a similar general meaning, as in the opening words of Nelson Mandela's first speech on his release from prison in 1990. Speaking to a crowd of over 50,000 in Cape Town, and many millions more on global television, he used two three-part lists consecutively.

Friends, comrades and fellow South Africans. I greet you all in the name of peace, democracy and freedom for all.

Contrastive pairs

Another common feature of political speeches is what Atkinson calls the contrastive pair, and what classical Greek and Roman writers on rhetoric called antithesis. Whereas the three-part list contains three parts which essentially complement each other, the contrastive pair contains two parts which are in some ways in opposition, but in other ways use repetition to make the overall effect. A good example of this is Neil Armstrong's words when he became the first person to set foot on the moon in 1969.

The context of these famous words is worth exploring. For days, millions living in the part of the world that was politically aligned to the USA had been watching television, waiting for the moment when the first astronaut would set foot on the moon. As Neil Armstrong was seen bouncing along the moon's surface, they heard his first words:

One small step for man: one giant leap for mankind.

These words show a range of repetition and contrast across the two parts of the utterance. The repeated 'one' is attached to words with contrasting meaning within the same semantic fields – 'small'/'giant' and 'step'/ 'leap'. The first words in each pair – 'small' and 'step' – are literal in that they describe what he was doing at the time, but the second words are metaphorical, 'giant leap' referring to technological progress. So 'for man' in one half becomes 'for mankind' in the second. Each part also has an identical syntactical structure, which although conveying a sense of an action has no main verb. There is also a phonological sense of repetition too, not just because some words are actually repeated but because the rhythm and stress are identical in each part.

The use of contrast and repetition, then, can involve a number of linguistic features: it can include lexical repetition; semantic repetition and/or contrast including the literal contrasted with the metaphorical; syntactical repetition; and phonological repetition. When looking this closely at Armstrong's words it also becomes clear that they were almost certainly scripted in advance; their patterns seem too neat for a spontaneous utterance. They are also, of course, very political, especially when they are put in the context of the so-called 'space race' going on at the time between the USA and the Soviet Union.

Nelson Mandela, continuing the speech quoted earlier in this unit said:

(a) 'I stand before you not as a prophet but as a humble servant of you, the people ... We have waited too long for our freedom. We can no longer wait.' (For commentary, see below.)

Margaret Thatcher, when elected to power for the first time in 1979, paraphrased, as part of her victory speech, the words of St Francis of Assisi. She said:

(b) 'Where there is discord, may we bring harmony.
Where there is error, may we bring truth.
Where there is doubt, may we bring faith.
Where there is despair, may we bring hope.'

In the run-up to the 1997 election in Britain, rising crime rates became an issue between the two major parties. The Conservative Party, then in power, claimed that it was tougher in its policies on crime than Labour would be. Tony Blair, for the Labour Party, replied that they would be:

(c)   'Tough on crime and tough on the causes of crime.'

Activity

Write a paragraph on each of the extracts from speeches quoted above (a, b, c), showing clearly how the speaker has used repetition and contrast. In addition to identifying the words or phrases which distinguish each part of the contrast, show how other language features also contribute to the overall effect.

Commentary

(a)   'I stand before you not as a prophet but as a humble servant of you, the people . . . We have waited too long for our freedom. We can no longer wait.'

There are two contrasts here. In the first, Mandela contrasts 'not being a prophet', with 'being a humble servant' – the negative coming before the positive as it usually does with pairs, so that the stress can be on the positive second part. He denies any special powers that would belong to a prophet, such as religious insight and foresight, and offers himself instead as a humble servant. Politicians often claim humility and service to the people as their motive for wanting power, but these are not particularly exciting qualities – it can be argued that in rejecting the role of prophet, Mandela has nonetheless planted the idea that he might be one, or that some see him as one. The grammatical cohesion of the contrast is achieved through the phrases 'not as/but as'.

In his second contrast quoted here, Mandela uses pronouns, verbs, adverbials of time and a negative to create the comparison, along with a subtle use of word order. The pronouns 'we/our' bind speaker to audience; agreement with his view is taken for granted. 'We have waited' (past tense, suggesting time right up to the present) 'too long' (adverbial) is contrasted with 'We can no longer wait.' As the message he wanted to give was one about peaceful but necessary change rather than instant and violent revolution, the word order becomes vital. The repeated verb 'wait' comes last — we have had to wait for it, because Mandela wants to put it at the most important place in the sentence — at the end ('for freedom' is not repeated but is understood).

(b) 'Where there is discord, may we bring harmony.
Where there is error, may we bring truth.
Where there is doubt, may we bring faith.
Where there is despair, may we bring hope.'

The contrasting pairs of abstract nouns — discord/harmony; error/ truth; doubt/faith; despair/hope — have a biblical ring to them, as you might expect from their source. St Francis, though, was talking about spiritual matters rather than politics and doubt/faith are perhaps hardest to apply in a political context, so the real emphasis lies with the last contrast, and especially the word 'hope' — which as an abstract noun suggests a bright future from a leader as she starts her term of office.

The contrasting abstract nouns are united by the repeated structures 'where there is' and 'may we bring', each repetition adding a weight of expectation. 'May we bring' is an unusual verb construction. It sounds very much like a prayer to a higher authority, although in fact the higher authority is Thatcher herself who has just gained power. In apparently seeking the help of an implied god, she is at the same time asserting her own power.

(c) 'Tough on crime and tough on the causes of crime.'

The contrast here is established by the addition of 'the causes of'. This time the contrast is not so much about the rejection of one thing for another, but the connection of two things, signalled by the conjunction 'and'. This soundbite gains added effect by the use of as few words as possible, even if meaning is ultimately obscured. It begins with the adjective 'tough' rather than naming the agents of toughness — the Labour Party. Presumably it is criminals, rather than crime, that will be treated toughly, but the repetition is more important than strict meaning. Likewise, you cannot literally be tough on the causes of crime, which are, by implication, social deprivation. You can aim to alleviate deprivation, but you cannot punish it. The aim is to suggest that Labour policy is more wide-ranging than that of the Conservatives, and that it will look at causes as well as effects; the word 'tough' carries most weight because it is placed first and repeated.

This soundbite, then, is a slogan representing a policy rather than a statement of the policy itself, which requires far more subtlety and detail. Soundbites require economy of expression: they need to be brief, yet using language structures which encourage them to be often repeated and easily remembered. Particularly popular in recent times has been the verb-less sentence, like the one used in (c) above; in one speech made to his party conference in 1998, Tony Blair used over a hundred of these.

Text : This England

> THIS ENGLAND
>
> Left alone, I drifted into the hall to find shadow health minister Chris Smith announcing that a Labour gov-ernment would ban tobacco advertising. Good for him.
> 'If you are ill or injured,' said Smith, 'if your health is damaged or under threat, there will be a National Health Service with the resources and the will to help . . .
> 'We will restore it.
> 'That's our promise.
> 'I repeat that: We will restore it. You will have a National Health Service again.
> 'Ask me why you should vote Labour. That reason will do alone. You will have a National Health Service again.'
> Cue applause. Me, I went to the press centre to get a copy of the speech and to check I was hearing right. Sure enough, large chunks of Smith's speech, and of every speech I had heard subsequently, seemed to have been written by an idiot.
> An idiot who couldn't handle paragraphs longer than a sentence. Who didn't like sentences with verbs in.
> Who liked his sentences . . .
> Really short.
> Well — I'm sure Smith's no idiot. I also heard Brown, Cook and Blair, and I'm sure they're not idiots either; Cook, indeed, was universally deemed to have a brain not the size of one planet but of several. So I just wonder if it isn't enormously frustrating for intel-ligent people to have to reduce difficult and complex subjects into morse code.
> So they can sound good on TV.
> But that's politics now.
> Reducing the world to the verbal equivalent of canapés.

Activity

The above extract is taken from *This England* (1997) by Pete Davies. Davies spent a year in a Yorkshire constituency observing the run-up to the 1997 British election. In this extract he has gone with the candidate to the Labour Party conference in Blackpool.

1   What is Davies' main point about contemporary speeches in this extract?
2   How does he reflect this view in his own writing?

There is no commentary with this activity.

We are a grandmother

When Margaret Thatcher announced on the steps of 10 Downing Street that her son and his wife had had a baby, she said, 'We are a grandmother.' This led to considerable mockery at the time because not only did it sound strange grammatically, but she had used what is known as the 'royal we'. Traditionally kings and queens of England have used this pronoun to refer to themselves, rather than the more personal 'I': it gives their utterances a more formal ring and perhaps also suggests that in their role as monarch they are talking for their people as well as themselves. When Margaret Thatcher used the word 'we', she was seen as giving herself royal airs, as being too self-important. The effect was especially pronounced because she was talking about family news rather than anything which affected the country as a whole. A similar effect can result from the use of the very impersonal pronoun 'one', instead of I. Although 'one' is still used by members of the royal family, and sometimes by others in high office, its very distancing effect means it is no longer popular with politicians who are trying to communicate that they are with the people in all that they do.

The pronouns politicians use in their speeches are worth looking at because they make a significant contribution to the overall effect. In terms of personal reference, there are essentially five ways politicians can introduce a measure that they intend to implement:

1   They can use the first person singular pronoun 'I': 'Today I intend to reduce taxes by 20 per cent.'
2   They can use the first person plural pronoun 'we': 'Today we intend to raise taxes by a mere 5 per cent.'

3   They can refer to their position: 'The Chancellor must raise taxes for the long-term good of the nation's economy' or their role as part of the government: ' The government must raise taxes . . .'

4   They can use no agentive pronoun at all, and instead use the agentless passive, where no direct responsibility for action is given: 'Today it has been found necessary to raise taxes by 20 per cent'

5   They can use a form of metonymy by making what they have created – their budget – into an agent itself: 'This budget will help all those on low incomes.'

Ignoring for the moment numbers 3-5, where no pronouns of responsibility are used, this means that when politicians make speeches, they have two sets of first person pronouns available. They can talk in the first person singular, using I/me/myself/mine or they can talk in the first person plural using we/us/ourselves/ours. The first person plural forms can have a range of reference:

- they can refer to 'I' plus one other; i.e. we = minister + prime minister
- they can refer to 'I' plus a group; i.e. we = minister + government and/or political party
- they can refer to 'I' plus the whole country; i.e. we = minister + people of Britain
- they can even refer to 'I' plus the rest of humanity; i.e. we = minister + people everywhere

The advantage of the singular forms (I/me/myself/mine) is that they show a clear sense of personal involvement on the part of the speaker, which is especially useful when good news is delivered. The disadvantage can be that they show all too clearly where blame lies if something goes wrong. They can also be seen as too self-important, with the individual speakers placing themselves above or outside the collective responsibility of their colleagues. The advantage of the plural pronoun forms (we/us/ourselves/ours) are that they help share the responsibility, especially when the decisions are tricky, when the news is uncertain. In their broadest reference they can show the politician in touch with all of the country, even all of the world. The disadvantage is that the individual does not gain so much credit when things go well.

    Pronouns are very common in talk, giving agency to actions (saying who is doing something) and helping to provide cohesion to the overall speech. Politicians and their speech writers, then, have some difficult decisions to make when it comes to using the pronouns that will keep appearing in their speeches: how much responsibility are they prepared to take on themselves; how much responsibility for success are they willing to share with other colleagues; how confident are they that whole groups of people share their views; how much responsibility for failure are they prepared to accept as their own? (See also the reference to transitivity in Unit 2.)

In reality they very often use a mixture of singular and plural pronouns, but analysing just which ones they use, and where, can give considerable insight into what they are saying and how they want to be viewed.

The British Chancellor of the Exchequer, Gordon Brown, opened his 1998 budget speech with the following words:

> Only once in a generation is the tax system fundamentally re-formed. The budget I bring before the house and country today begins the task of modernising not just taxation but the entire tax and benefit systems of our country. We do this to encourage enterprise; to reward work; to support families; to advance the ambitions not just of the few but of the many.

At first reading/hearing it may well be some of the more obvious features of political speech-making that you notice: the use of vocabulary that is very strong in meaning ('only once'/'fundamentally'/'entire'); the repeated reference to 'country'; a four-part list which seems to lack the potency of a three-parter; the contrastive pair of 'few'/'many'. But what has also been introduced in this speech is a variation of use of first person pronouns. While it is 'I' who is speaking to the house and country, it is 'we' who are encouraging and rewarding by making fundamental changes.

In the rest of his speech (not quoted here), Gordon Brown used first person singular pronouns in roughly equal numbers to first person plural, where 'we' stood for him + his government colleagues. He tended to use singular forms (I/me) in two ways: (1) to refer to successful action already taken – 'The plan I put in place last July is not only on track but is being achieved more quickly than expected.' (2) to announce policies which will be popular – 'Today I announce a tax cut for hundreds of thousands of working families on low income.' Plural forms, where 'we' stood for him + his government colleagues, tended to be in less prominent parts of the speech and often followed a series of singular forms: 'In the last budget I cut the small companies' tax rate from 23p to 21p. I have now decided to go further. From April small companies tax will be cut again to 20p. And we will also keep this rate ... for the whole Parliament.'

Gordon Brown also frequently used 'we', meaning him + the people of Britain: 'we must break for good from the conflicts and dogmas that have held us back and for too long have failed our country.' On these occasions he tended to talk in very general terms, often referring to abstract ideas rather than specific policies or policy changes. At the same time words like 'country', 'Britain', 'nation' were used to make the pronoun reference to 'we' absolutely clear: 'We must build a national economic purpose around new ambitions for Britain.'

Activity

The following text forms the last part of Gordon Brown's budget speech in 1998 (it has been slightly edited). This speech, although made in Parliament, was in many ways addressed also to the people of Britain, because it was broadcast live, and many soundbites later appeared in news broadcasts.

1   Investigate the way Brown uses pronouns in this speech.
2   Which parts of the speech would make suitable soundbites?
3   This is the end of a long speech. In what ways does Brown try to finish with impact and emphasis? Look in particular at what he says and how he says it, referring if possible to some of the features already referred to in this unit.

Text: Budget Speech

NB: Although this speech was scripted in advance, it was written to be spoken. This means that punctuation and paragraphing, which help give the appearance of a written text, are in fact added to help the reader. No record is made here of any pauses or hesitations which may have naturally occurred.

'We are determined to improve education all round. So I am allocating for the coming year to education an additional £250 million. Making a total additional commitment to education since we came to power of £2.5 billion . . .

The extra money I announced last July for the NHS comes on stream from next month. I have decided that this allocation to health of £1.2 billion for next year should today be increased by another £500 million to £1.7 billion. This takes the total additional investment we have provided for the NHS in our first 10 months to £2 billion. The NHS is safe in this government's hands.

Because we will always be prudent, I am allocating £500 million to add to the reserve in 1998-99. It is because of our prudence that we are able to meet our manifesto commitments, reduce the deficit and invest more in transport, education and health. The ambitions of the British people are once again the ambitions of the British government. So this is a budget that, by its measures, advances both enterprise and fairness. A budget that has set new ambitions for Britain.

I commend it to the House.'

Commentary

Although Brown begins by affirming that 'we', the government, are committed to education, he then says that 'I' am allocating extra funds. Politicians enjoy quoting figures when they suit their cause, so here he not only mentions the extra money for this year, but the total extra money so far. The same process operates with increased money for the Health Service (NHS): first he refers to last year's increase, then announces that 'I have decided' to add even more.

Having said that 'I' will give more to health, he moves to 'we have provided' and then the metaphorical 'The NHS is safe in this government's hands.' The metaphor of safe hands is interesting here; only one pair of hands can hold the baby, so at the very same time that he is talking about his government colleagues and a shared responsibility for the good news that he is giving, he is at the same time conjuring an image of one person – the safe hands are his.

One possible soundbite at this point is: 'I am allocating for the coming year to education an additional £250 million.' This rather strange word order when written – the sum of money would normally come after 'allocating' – allows more emphasis on the sum of money when spoken, because it comes at the end of the utterance. A similar effect is created when he announces more money for health: 'I have decided that this allocation to health of £1.2 billion for next year should today be increased by another £500 million to £1.7 billion.' The contrast between 'next year' and 'today' also gives added emphasis. 'The NHS is safe in this government's hands' has all the hallmarks of a conscious soundbite, written into the speech to be taken out again. It is short, metaphorical and definite in what it says.

Once he becomes more general and more abstract in his language, he talks consistently about 'we'. In repeating the word 'ambitions' (which, incidentally, he used four times at the beginning of his speech) he sets up a pair of likeness between the ambitions of the 'British people' and the ambitions of the 'British government'. By inserting 'once again' there is a clear pointer that this had not been the case with the previous government: the new government is returning to policies which unite government and people in a way that the previous government did not do. To make sure that this point is clearly made, 'ambitions' is repeated a third time – 'new ambitions for Britain'.

Because this is the end of a long speech – Brown spoke uninterrupted for over an hour – it needs to have some impact, to give a sense of something ending on a high note. Leaving what are highly popular measures to the very end, such as more money for education and health, is one method. So too is repeating the word 'ambitions' which he had used so prominently from the start. This gives the speech a sense of shape, of its various parts being in harmony, although only those who had listened attentively throughout would see the connection.

Something is also needed for those who have not heard the whole speech, and for broadcasters who want short soundbites. This is achieved through a pattern of repetition and something very similar to a three-part list. It works as follows, with each part, or all of it, a possible soundbite:

1   Ambitions of people = ambitions of government.
2   This budget is enterprising and fair.
3   This budget sets new ambitions for Britain.

Repeated words and/or ideas are: ambitions; people/Britain; this budget. He ends the actual speech with the word 'Britain', placing the greatest emphasis on the nation.

The final words form part of the conventions of parliamentary debate, but Brown ends on a personal note. It is his budget, so 'I commend it' rather than 'we'.

In conclusion, then, this short extract from a much longer speech shows how modern politicians have to construct speeches that hold together through their entire length by using various repeated words, ideas and structures, but at the same time how they must be aware of the need for highlights which can be taken out of context and used as soundbites.

Lend me your ears

Political speeches are as old as politics itself, and given that the word 'politics' comes from the Greek word for 'city'/'government', it should be no surprise that the Greeks studied the art of rhetoric and wrote manuals on how to persuade an audience.

Shakespeare at his grammar school would have studied rhetoric, and he put this to use when writing his play *Julius Caesar*. After the death of Caesar, Mark Antony speaks to the crowd, who have been persuaded by Brutus that Caesar deserved to die. He is in a dangerous position, for he too is seeking power, but he wants to gain it by raising sorrow and then anger at the death of Caesar. If Brutus can be disgraced, then he can step into the power vacuum.

Activity

Read carefully these opening lines from Antony's speech and comment on its persuasive qualities. In particular think about (a) how Shakespeare uses techniques noted earlier in this unit and (b) how repetition is used to create a sense of persuasion.

Text : Julius Caesar

> Friends, Romans, countrymen, lend me your ears;
> I come to bury Caesar, not to praise him.
> The evil that men do lives after them,
> The good is oft interred with their bones;
> So let it be with Caesar. The noble Brutus
> Hath told you Caesar was ambitious.
> If it were so, it was a grievous fault,
> And grievously hath Caesar answer'd it.
> Here, under leave of Brutus and the rest,
> (For Brutus is an honourable man,
> So are they all, all honourable men)
> Come I to speak in Caesar's funeral.
> He was my friend, faithful and just to me;
> But Brutus says he was ambitious,
> And Brutus is an honourable man.
> He hath brought many captives home to Rome,
> Whose ransoms did the general coffers fill;
> Did this in Caesar seem ambitious?

Commentary

This speech is part of a play, and is written in blank verse, but many of the features already noted in this unit can be seen. Remember that Shakespeare wrote the lines, not Antony, but within the context of the play Antony is trying to persuade an angry mob to change their view. He begins with a three-part list ('friends'/'Romans'/'countrymen') – and follows it with two contrastive pairs ('bury'/'not praise and evil'/ 'good').

There is considerable repetition in the speech, especially around the names of Caesar and Brutus. The intention in this repetition, which continues beyond this extract, is to persuade the crowd that Caesar was unjustly murdered and that Brutus is to blame. The words 'The noble Brutus/Hath...told you Caesar was ambitious', while appearing to praise Brutus, suggest that there could be a difference between what has been said by Brutus and what is fact. The repetition of the words 'Brutus is an honourable man' also undermines at the very same time it seems to praise. The second time these words are used follows a key line: 'He was my friend', faithful and just to me'. In repeating the idea of friendship that he used right at the start, and following it with 'faithful and just', Antony is suggesting that what Brutus says is wrong. The connective 'But' carries a great deal of weight here, suggesting that there is a difference between what Antony says about Caesar and what Brutus has said about him. By the time the actor playing Antony reaches the words 'Brutus is an honourable man' for the second time (and indeed the third and fourth, which follow this extract) they will carry, in their ironic intonation, the effect of a marvellous soundbite.

This extract ends with a **rhetorical question**, a question that is not expected to be answered. Having told the people that Caesar brought money into the economy – always popular – he then returns to the claim about ambition, asking whether Caesar can be ambitious when he did such good for others. The implied, but unstated answer is 'no'. Antony, who later claims that he is 'no orator', has used language to manipulate his audience into completely reversing their previous thoughts.

Activity

This unit has focused on four main aspects of political speech-making: the soundbite/claptrap; the list of three; contrastive pairs; use of pronouns. In this final activity, extracts are printed from two speeches made in similar circumstances. The first is by Liberal Democrats leader Paddy Ashdown, who was addressing his party in advance of the 1997 General Election, and the second by Tony Blair, opening his party's campaign in the same election. In each case the extracts have been slightly abridged. They are printed in the form they were issued as press releases.

Write your own commentary on these extracts, showing examples of the four aspects named above, and how each politician uses the rhetoric of persuasion – including the use of metaphor, as discussed in Unit 2 – to prepare their supporters and potential voters for the election to come.

Text: Paddy Ashdown

'Believe me: there are millions of people – who believe, privately, in all that you and I believe in. Who want to help build that more prosperous nation with a more generous heart.

There is a majority of people in this country who believe in fairness, in generosity, in self-sufficiency.

Who love this country and its people and who long for a greater sense of pride and purpose.

Who look for wise guidance for themselves and their children.

And who desperately hope that someone, somewhere, will see where the sun is shining on the fields ahead – and show them the path to get there.

We have within our sights the achievement of all we stand for.

A victory for principle, a victory for persistence.

A victory that will give a new shape to hope and new opportunity to every single person in this country.

A victory that will make all our long years of commitment, persistence and endeavour all the sweeter.

It can be won.

I know it can be won.

And I know that you can win it.'

Text: Tony Blair

'We are the party of practical ideas today. The Tories are the party of outdated dogma.

We are the party of the decent, hardworking majority. The Tories the party of extremes.

We are the party that can unify the nation and bring it together. The Tories are the party that divide it.

People see surveys showing businessmen and women increasingly turning to Labour and they know New Labour is real.

Our campaign will be New Labour

Our manifesto will be New Labour

And if elected our government will be New Labour.

What the Tories cannot stand is that the policies we set out are popular, practical and in touch with the British People.

We do not promise a revolution. We promise a government which can bring the country together, heal the divisions of the past and look to the future with pride and with confidence. We promise only what we will deliver and we will deliver what we promise.

In the weeks ahead we will lay our case before the British people ... on May 1st it is the people who must decide who they wish to lead Britain into the next millennium.'

Extension

1 Read the full text of Antony's speech (Act III, Scene 2 of *Julius Caesar*) and examine how he continues to manipulate his audience until they support his cause.

2 Analysing political speeches can lead to interesting research projects. It is, though, a very large field of research; speeches are made every day across the world and you cannot possibly cover them all. Instead you need to find a sharp focus. This might involve some of the following:

   (a) Investigating the major speeches one politician makes during a campaign.

(b)   Comparing the speeches made by two rivals in a campaign. It can be especially interesting to do this when the rivals belong to the same political party, and are therefore both allies and enemies. On the other hand, you could compare two central but equivalent figures of opposite parties.

(c)   Comparing speeches made by English-speaking politicians from different countries.

(d)   Investigating speeches made in specific contexts, such as parliaments, where there are rules and conventions that limit what can be said.

Winning elections: slogans and posters

In a democratic nation, to gain power you must win elections. Persuading people to vote for you is a vital part of the political process. As has been seen in Unit 2, politics often shares a vocabulary with military activity, and this is especially the case with elections: both winning elections and winning wars involve running successful campaigns.

From a linguistic point of view political campaigns are of interest because they show language being used for such a clear and central purpose. Although political campaigns, with their speeches, their written texts, their broadcasts, need to inform and instruct voters about issues that are considered to be of great importance, ultimately all the written and spoken texts that are produced during an election campaign are designed to persuade people to do one thing: to vote in a certain way.

Just how this persuasive purpose is carried out varies hugely, ranging from so-called negative campaigning, where candidates attack opponents rather then sell themselves, to more positive methods where candidates, usually not yet in power, sell themselves as a brand new product, much better than the old one that is currently being used. Language is a vital part of this process of selling, but not the only one. Television is generally seen as the most important part of the political battleground, and party broadcasts and/or advertisements, paid for by the political parties, are often sophisticated media productions produced by high-profile film directors.

In this unit a number of persuasive texts will be looked at. They do not give the full picture of how politicians sell themselves, but they do show how linguistic techniques of persuasion contribute to the process.

Party slogans

Many organisations and institutions, such as public services like hospitals and the police, educational institutions like schools and colleges, and commercial companies selling products and services, now incorporate a logo and slogan into their corporate identity. This means that when the name of the institution/company is written, it is (a) accompanied by (or even replaced by) a logo which symbolically represents an idea that we are meant to associate with the institution/company, and (b) followed by a slogan which briefly and, it is hoped, memorably suggests something about the work of the institution or the product the company makes. These slogans are constructed to catch the attention of readers and make them think. They often do so by playing with words and meaning, and simply by having a slogan an organisation can be seen as making a claim for status; the words it uses will aim to give a positive view of the organisation's work.

Activity

Slogans are devised to sell products and institutions, so not surprisingly political parties use them as part of their persuasive package: they appear on posters, party broadcasts and wherever the parties are advertising themselves. The following are all slogans used by parties in the British election of 1997. Group the slogans in as many ways as you can, and say what the linguistic connections are within each group. For instance you will find some which: have similar grammatical structures; make reference to time, either directly or by implication; refer to place; contain double meanings, deliberate or otherwise.

Labour (Leading opposition party)

New Labour		equipping Britain for the future
new hope	new life for Britain	

because Britain deserves better because you deserve better enough is enough

Britain will be better with New Labour

It's up to you
A choice of two futures

Conservative (Government party)

Britain is booming
Don't throw it away   You can only be sure with the Conservatives
Think before you vote

Liberal Democrats (Second opposition party)

choose Liberal Democrats   make the difference

Liberal Democrats
Making the difference

Green Party

Invest in your future   Vote Green for policies which won't cost you the
earth

Pro-Life Alliance (Anti-Abortion)

Make the right choice

Referendum Party (Anti-EEC)

Let the people decide
Put country before party

British National Party (Nationalist Neo-fascist)

Protest
For a real change vote BNP

Scottish National Party

Yes We Can - Win the Best for Scotland

Commentary

There is no right answer to this activity and you may well have come up
with groupings which are not mentioned below. The commentary which
follows is longer than some others in this book because these slogans
highlight a number of linguistic features which are worth looking for in
other data you may collect.

One group which is easily recognised involves those which contain a command verb form: 'Don't throw it away'; 'choose Liberal Democrats'; 'make the difference'; 'Invest in your future'; 'Vote Green . . . '; 'Make the right choice'; 'Let the people decide'; 'Put country before party'; 'Protest . . . vote BNP' and 'Win the Best for Scotland'.

Another easily identified group involves reference to place: 'new life for Britain'; 'because Britain deserves better'; 'equipping Britain for the future'; 'Britain will be better with New Labour'; 'Britain is booming'; 'Win the Best for Scotland'; 'Put country before party' and 'Vote Green for policies which won't cost you the earth'. All of these, except the last one, suggest a call to patriotism, of putting your country before self. The Green Party slogan, though, suggests we must vote not to save the country but the whole planet.

When one party is in power already, and others want to gain power, it is not surprising that slogans refer to time, either directly or by implication. 'Don't throw it away' suggests 'keep what you have had and still have now'. Two slogans on the other hand refer directly to the future, and one to two futures. Other slogans imply time and change: all the Labour slogans carry this suggestion, with the words 'new' (different from old) 'better' (than it is now) and 'enough is enough' (it's time to start again).

Deliberate play with meaning occurs in two slogans. 'Vote Green for policies which won't cost you the earth' has two meanings for 'cost you the earth': one means that a Green vote will not cost you money in terms of expensive policies, the second that a green vote will not lead to the destruction of the environment. 'Make the right choice' has two meanings for 'choice': one is the way you choose to vote; the other involves not choosing to abort unborn children - although presumably the party does not actually want women to have the chance to choose.

'Make the right choice' also carries a further, unintended meaning. The word 'right' is associated with a political stance (see Unit 1), usually suggesting narrow social views; although many would feel that to vote Pro-Life Alliance is indeed to vote for a right-wing party, it is unlikely that the slogan was devised with that in mind. Similarly, 'You can only be sure with the Conservatives' carries an unintended meaning. Presumably the intention is that sureness and certainty come from the Conservatives, who had after all at that time been in power for so long. It is suggested that this is not the case with other (deliberately) unnamed parties. In English the word 'only' can be problematic, however, its place in a sentence technically governing what it refers to. Even if this usage is no longer adhered to strictly, some readers might still have puzzled over the slogan: does it mean that you can be sure with the Conservatives but no other party, or does it mean that you can experience sureness with the Conservatives but nothing else?

Ambiguity and implication have already been seen in the groups above, but another way of categorising these features is to look at grammatical structures. These are slogans, which by definition must be brief, and brevity is achieved in a number of ways. One way is by the use of noun phrases, and nothing else. So 'new hope', 'new life for Britain', 'a choice of two futures' are phrases rather than complete sentences. They work by using implicature: the reader has to supply the 'full' meaning. 'New life for Britain', for instance, would in full read something like 'vote Labour and you will find that life in Britain will improve' - a sentence that carries far less impact than the single noun phrase standing alone.

Omitting words, making statements deliberately brief, is called **ellipsis**. The way pronouns are used is another example. Usually pronouns have reference to something that has gone before, but in some of these slogans that does not happen. 'It's up to you' and 'Don't throw it away' use the pronoun 'it' without any explicit reference. This creates a deliberate ambiguity, but also makes the reader think - what is 'it'? In the Labour slogan it could refer to the future of the country, or the result of the election or more probably both. In the Conservative slogan it refers to past success, success that has been hard fought for, but which could easily be lost with the wrong vote.

The pronouns 'you'/'your' also appear frequently, and again they contain ambiguity. In English, 'you' is both singular and plural (unlike the French *tu / vous*). This means that 'You can only be sure . . .' and 'It's up to you' are addressing both you as an individual, the person with the single vote, but also you as part of a whole country's population, who should all be working together. This slogan, as with many others in this selection, carries reminders of slogans that have gone before and a shared awareness we have of them. 'Your country needs you', one of the best known of all British political slogans, made exactly the same use of this unreferenced 'you'.

The Scottish Nationalists are the only party to use the pronoun 'we', which is also ambiguous in its reference. The first part of its hyphenated slogan says 'Yes We Can', the 'we' referring either to them as a party, or to everybody together. Perhaps because they are speaking to a regional group, rather than the whole of Britain, they are more able to suggest an assumption that all are in this together. They are assuming a common identity rather than appealing for it, an effect which is emphasised by the affirmative 'yes'. The whole phrase is also elliptical, because the **modal verb** 'can' is left on its own, rather than being followed by another verb. 'Yes We Can', with its reinforcing capital letters, is an open answer to any question - we can do anything that we want or you ask.

The **comparative** form 'better' is used in three Labour slogans. The elliptical effect here is achieved by using a comparative form, but not making an actual comparison - better than what? Once again the reader has to supply this. The advantage of not making the comparison is that it allows each reader to supply their own mental picture of what might be better — certainly better than we have now, but in unspecified ways. Meanwhile the Scottish Nationalists (SNP) use the **superlative** 'best'. Whereas the Labour Party slogans imply they are competing against the government in power, the SNP are taking on all-comers.

Two of the slogans mentioned in the paragraph above begin with the word 'because', and there is also an elliptical effect here. A **conjunction** is a word that joins together two clauses, and 'because' is a causal conjunction: two things are related through cause and effect. 'Because' can be positioned either in the middle of the two clauses - 'she voted Green because she wanted to save the environment'- or at the beginning - 'Because he was fed up with all the parties, he decided not to vote'. In the two slogans 'because Britain deserves better'/ 'because you deserve better', the other part of the causal relationship is omitted and so must be supplied by the reader. There is considerable scope for ambiguity here, especially as the slogans could come before the omitted clause or after it. Undoubtedly one clause the reader is meant to supply is 'vote Labour', but the slogan works more effectively by this being just one option among many. Both of these slogans, incidentally, were placed alongside clear visual clues that this was a Labour Party poster, just in case the reader supplied a message that included voting for someone else - ambiguity works well in creating a message, but must not be so strong that the reader is free to miss the point entirely.

'Equipping Britain for the future' and 'Making the difference' both use the '-ing' form of a verb; this is one of the most popular forms in company and organisational slogans. The effect again depends on ellipsis, because the verb is without an **agent** - we are not told explicitly *who* is equipping/making, although we can work it out easily enough. In addition to there being no agent there is also no **aspect,** because the verb is timeless, without end. The equipping/making are continuous, unbroken and so, by implication, going on forever. These slogans, therefore, could also be placed with those others that more explicitly refer to time.

Party posters

One of the most visually striking ways in which political parties sell themselves during an election is by using posters. Many of these are placed on advertising billboards, and for the duration of the campaign we are encouraged to buy a political party rather than the soft drink or chocolate bar that usually occupies this space. The political parties buy billboard space because, although we can switch off their election broadcasts or throw away their leaflets unread, it is very hard for us to ignore the huge signs that surround us in our everyday environment. In many ways the parties use the techniques of selling a product to sell themselves to us.

As texts, political posters must do certain things. They must catch our attention and hold it long enough for the message to be taken in. This means that they must be visually eye-catching and must not take long to read - especially as many are placed strategically along busy roads. The amount of verbal text is bound to be limited, but it will be phrased to make an impact on the reader. Sometimes a series of posters is released, either at the same time, or in sequence so that the public become used to a certain format.

The posters overleaf were all part of a campaign by Labour in the run-up to the 1997 election, and are notable because apart from the use of various colours, rather than the traditional red, they largely consist of words alone.

Activity

Obviously each poster is addressing a different issue, but at the same time as a series they have features in common. Make brief notes on (a) how these posters establish a 'brand identity' for Labour, and (b) how they can be grouped according to their linguistic features. Use the discussion of logos above to help you here. Finally, share your responses with a partner if possible.

Text: General Election 1997 billboard posters

YOUNG
OFFENDERS WILL
BE PUNISHED

Labour

MORE JOBS
FOR
YOUNG PEOPLE

Labour

NHS WAITING
LISTS WILL
BE SHORTER

Labour

CLASS SIZES
WILL
BE SMALLER

Labour

INCOME TAX
RATES
WILL NOT RISE

Labour

BRITAIN
DESERVES
BETTER

Labour

Commentary

Visually, each poster has three lines of text in large block print. The 'product' is identified simply as Labour along with its logo, a single rose. This is in smaller print and is usually centred at the bottom of the poster.

Three of the posters include unreferenced comparatives - 'better', 'smaller', 'shorter'. Four of the posters contain 'will', and three the words 'will be'. The words 'will be' are not used in the same way though; 'will be smaller' and 'will be shorter' are active verbs followed by comparatives, whereas 'will be punished' is a passive structure. The use of passive forms allows the agent to remain unidentified: who will do the punishing is not mentioned. The final use of 'will' is as a modal verb in 'will not rise'. In all cases 'will' can be read in two ways: without emphasis it can signify the future; or with emphasis it can suggest something definite that is going to happen.

All the texts except 'more jobs for young people', which is a phrase, are simple sentences. Because the comparative 'more' comes first, it would take too many words to complete a full sentence, which would have to be something like 'there will be more jobs for young people.' Reversing the order and saying 'young people will have more jobs' would alter the sense, suggesting that an actual promise is being made to all young people. Of all the posters this is the one which grammatically is most out of place, but it visually follows the pattern of the others, which is more important to the series as a whole.

Saints and demons

The posters looked at above are relatively unusual in that they rely solely upon words to get their message across. More typically, election campaign posters include significant visual material too. Increasingly this includes representations of leading political figures, especially the party leaders themselves. As with other aspects of the campaign, political parties tend to do one of two things: they either represent their own leader, in which case the poster is designed to show this person in an impressive light; or they portray their opponents, in which case they are shown in ways which ridicule them. The extent of this ridicule is a matter of fine judgement and it can sometimes backfire on the party which produces it.

Early in the British campaign of 1997, the Conservative Party, worried by the personal popularity of Tony Blair, attempted to undermine Blair's image by suggesting that behind the pleasant façade lay a dangerous man. Their 'Demon Eyes' campaign, which showed a pair of glowing red eyes peeping from behind velvet curtains represented visually this idea of danger lurking behind a smooth exterior. The posters, though, had to be withdrawn mid-way through the campaign because opinion polls suggested that people were not responding to them in the way intended. Although the implied message was understood, it was not approved of or agreed with. Instead respondents felt that this was an unfair representation of Blair and that it showed that the Conservatives were resorting to character assassination in a desperate attempt to win votes. Far from helping the Conservative cause, it only hindered it further.

Activity

Each of the three posters printed below shows a visual representation of party leaders in the 1997 campaign. Text 1 shows the then Prime Minister John Major on a Labour poster. Text 2 shows Tony Blair on a Labour poster and Text 3 shows John Major and Tony Blair on a Liberal Democrats poster.

For Texts 1 and 3 work out how words and pictures combine to give a negative view of the figures involved. Say what form this negative message takes — what are the figures being accused of by their opponents?

Text 2 makes a direct link between Tony Blair himself and a slogan which has already been analysed earlier in this unit. How does this very carefully composed picture present a positive view of Blair?

Text 1: Enough is enough

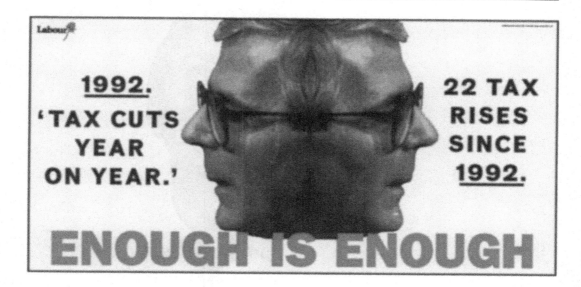

Text 2 : Billboards – Party Leaders

because Britain
deserves better

Labour

P/001/97 Published by the Labour Party, John Smith House, 150 Walworth Road, London SE17 1JT.
Designed by GIANT. Printed by H H Associates, Royal Crest House, 22-26 Upper Mulgrave Road, Cheam, Surrey SM2 7AZ.

Text 3 : Punch and Judy

Commentary

That Text 1 is issued by the Labour Party can be detected by the fact that the party logo appears on the poster, but it is placed in the top left-hand corner, and is in much smaller print than on most other Labour posters. This suggests that the producers of the text are less concerned with promoting themselves than with a negative portrayal of their main opponent. Just as Text 2 uses Tony Blair to represent Labour positively, so John Major is used here to represent his party negatively. In this sense it is a contest between leaders, between individuals, rather than a contest between parties or local candidates.

Visually, John Major is seen as two faces in profile, looking in different directions: this is a visual representation of the verbal phrase 'two-faced', meaning we are meant to see Major as untrust-worthy, a liar. The idea of 'two' is sustained by numerical and verbal means also: the year 1992 begins and ends the central part of the text; 'tax rises' are balanced by 'tax cuts'; the final slogan 'enough is enough' repeats the key word – it is time for change, and for fewer tax rises too.

Text 2 aims to give a positive representation of the party leader portrayed. This time we see the face full on, and it is given even more prominence by the slight cropping of the top of Blair's head. The smile is open, relaxed, confident, but the eyes look out beyond the picture, looking upwards to a vision - of a better future, perhaps, or even of some sort of divine assistance. This picture, which would have been carefully posed and chosen from hundreds of shots, nonetheless wants to give a sense of a man caught happily at his work. He has his sleeves rolled up - to roll your sleeves up is an idiom meaning to get stuck into work - and his tie loose. But he is wearing a tie, and his shirt is white and pressed: the touch of the informal is balanced by a man who wears clothes suitable for high office. This time the logo is much more prominent, and the slogan that has been used elsewhere is repeated here - 'because Britain deserves better.' As was noted earlier, this is just one half of a causal relationship, and so there is a deliberate ambiguity as to what should come before 'because'; in this case it is more personally directed at Tony Blair than at his party.

The third text, published by the Liberal Democrats, aims to ridicule the contest between the two leaders. In talking of 'the Punch and Judy Show' and representing Major and Blair as puppet figures, it suggests that the leaders are slugging out an old ritual with little relevance to the real issues. The reader is urged to 'make the difference' which carries at least two possible meanings: one is to vote Liberal Democrat for a change of power; the other that a vote for the Liberal Democrats is a vote against party leaders indulging in empty point-scoring politics.

In the first text, a party leader is represented by the opposition as a failure. In the second text, the same party represents its leader as a success. In the third text, both leaders are represented as fighting the wrong battle.

Analysis of texts related to election campaigns is continued in the next unit.

Winning elections: national and local manifestos

The previous unit looked at the language of slogans and posters, language that was essentially elliptical and designed to create an instant response. This unit will look at written campaign texts that are longer and more sustained in their attempts to persuade their audience to a certain point of view.

As part of the campaigning process in elections, political parties issue written statements of their policies and beliefs. The first part of this unit will look at the introductory sections to three of these statements, one American 'platform' and two British 'manifestos'.

Platform – the American Democratic Party

In August 1996, the Democratic National Convention adopted its National Platform for the presidential campaign leading to elections in November of that year. Bill Clinton, their candidate, was already in power, so this was an attempt to re-elect him for a second and final term of office. Although American parties are less clearly on the left/right divide than their British counterparts, the Democrats are traditionally seen as being to the left of their main opponents, the Republicans. The success of the Democratic campaign was closely observed by the British Labour Party in advance of their campaign in 1997.

Text: Democratic National Platform

THE 1996 DEMOCRATIC NATIONAL PLATFORM

Today's Democratic Party:
Meeting America's Challenges, Protecting America's Values

INTRODUCTION

In 1996, America will choose the President who will lead us from the millennium which saw the birth of our nation, and into a future that has all the potential to be even greater than our magnificent past. Today's Democratic Party is ready for that future. Our vision is simple. We want an America that gives all Americans the chance to live out their dreams and achieve their God-given potential. We want an America that is still the world's strongest force for peace and freedom. And we want an America that is coming together around our enduring values, instead of drifting apart.

Today's Democratic Party is determined to renew America's most basic bargain: Opportunity to every American, and responsibility from every American. And today's Democratic Party is determined to reawaken the great sense of American community.

Opportunity. Responsibility. Community. These are the values that made America strong. These are the values of the Democratic Party. These are the values that must guide us into the future.

Today, America is moving forward with the strong Presidential leadership it deserves. The economy is stronger, the deficit is lower, and government is smaller. Education is better, our environment is cleaner, families are healthier, and our streets are safer. There is more opportunity in America, more responsibility in our homes, and more peace in the world.

Today's Democratic Party stands proudly on the record of the last four years. We are living in an age of enormous possibility, and we are working to make sure that all Americans can make the most of it. America is moving in the right direction.

Now we must move forward, and we know the course we must follow. We need a smaller, more effective, more efficient, less bureaucratic government that reflects our time-honored values. The American people do not want big government solutions and they do not want empty promises. They want a government that is for them, not against them; that doesn't interfere with their lives but enhances their quality of life. They want a course that is reasonable, help that is realistic, and solutions that can be delivered – a moderate, achievable, common-sense agenda that will improve people's daily lives and not increase the size of government.

That is what today's Democratic Party offers: the end of an era of big government and a final rejection of the misguided call to leave our citizens to fend for themselves – and bold leadership into the future: To meet America's challenges, protect America's values, and fulfill American dreams.

Read the introduction to the Democratic National Platform on p. 74. Work out responses to the following task and then, if possible, share them with a partner or partners. When you have discussed your responses, write a short commentary on the text.

Task: Analyse the methods used in this text to persuade its readers, by looking in particular at:

(a) language features that are found in political speeches (see Unit 3), but which are present here in a written text.
(b) the way references to time operate in the text. How does the language used help to reinforce the idea that the Democrats are already in power and want to be elected for a further term?
(c) the use of pronouns in this text. Which are used frequently, and which are not used at all? Suggest some reasons for this.

One of the most striking features of this text is that it uses many of the language features identified in Unit 3 on political speeches. One reason for this might be that the text was adopted at the party's national convention, so to some extent it is meant to be heard as well as read. There are many examples of three-part lists: the third paragraph, for instance is built entirely around them, with three single-word sentences followed by three sentences that each begin with the phrase 'these are the values'. Contrastive pairs also appear, such as 'coming together'/ 'drifting apart', 'for them'/'not against them', 'do not want'/'want'. More generally, there is a considerable amount of repetition, especially of abstract nouns that name qualities which many voters would see as positive: 'peace', 'values', 'dreams', 'community'.

One particular **semantic field** that helps to give the text its cohesion involves references to time, with a strong sense of past, present and future being evoked. This is introduced in the slogan at the top of the text; it is not just the Democratic Party but 'Today's Democratic Party', implying that the party now is not necessarily the same party as it has been before. As well as forming part of an often repeated label, the word 'today' also represents a point on a metaphorical long journey that is only half-completed; 'Today, America is moving forward' with Clinton in power and half-way through his possible term of office, but also 'Now we must move forward, and we know the course we must follow.' A much wider sense of time is invoked in the opening paragraph of the text. Because Clinton's second term of office would end in the year 2000, there are references to 'the birth of our nation' and 'a future' millennium.

A party or president already in office faces a particular problem when fighting an election campaign; they have to look back enough to suggest that they have achieved plenty so far, but at the same time they have to suggest that they still have plenty of ideas for the future. The opening slogan, using the comparison of 'meeting challenges' with 'protecting values', carries the suggestion of time future and time past, and this careful balance between future success and past achievement is evident throughout. The text begins and ends looking to the future, because this is an attempt to gain another term of office, and in the middle makes reference to a successful, but in policy terms incomplete past. So comparative terms such as 'stronger', 'lower' and 'smaller' all imply improvement on the past and potential for yet more to come. The two paragraphs that specifically refer to the recent past (paragraphs four and five) are completed by the sentence 'America is moving in the right direction.' The verb form here is one of continuous action, which is picked up immediately in the next paragraph with 'Now we must move forward' heralding a change of perspective from looking back to looking forward again.

There are many references to America and Americans throughout the text: they are mentioned twice in the opening headline. The repeated references to the name of the country – or one version of it – are part of an appeal to patriotism and an ideology that constructs 'America' as a country with a 'magnificent past' and at the same time 'a future that has all the potential to be even greater'. Americans have 'dreams' and 'God-given potential' and their country is the 'world's strongest force for peace and freedom'. Much of the rhetoric here is about taking a very confident, positive and hopeful view of the country.

The danger with this approach, however, is that it may be seen as complacent, especially when the party saying these things is the party actually running the country. Many elections have been fought by parties in power on a so-called 'feel-good factor', but to admit that everything is fine and dandy runs a huge risk. Here, then, the constructed view of a country with a great past and even greater future is tempered by the admission that America is 'drifting apart' and that some basic bargains between government and people need to 'renewed'. Today's Democratic Party will be the party to 'reawaken' a sense of community.

An introductory statement such as this is essentially a rallying cry, so it is unlikely that any specific policies will be outlined yet. The paragraph which contains most in terms of political ideas is the penultimate one, and this paragraph is also useful as an example of the way pronoun reference works in this text. Because the readership will first be party members, and later a much wider audience, no direct reference is made to the reader at all – at no point are 'you' urged to do anything. Nor are there any first-person pronouns: this document has been written to support Bill Clinton, but not by him.

Instead there are references to 'we' and 'they', 'they' clearly standing for all American people. The reference of 'we' is particularly subtle here, especially in the first sentence of this paragraph. 'Now we must move forward' refers to the nation as a whole, whereas 'and we know the course we must follow' is more ambiguous, suggesting simultaneously both the nation and the party. This gives a sense of the nation and the party being identical, so when the paragraph goes on to describe what the American people want it is implied that this is what the party wants and will deliver. The opening of the final paragraph reinforces this point. The fact that the people want apparently contradictory things – a government that doesn't interfere, yet one that makes their lives better – is masked partly by the rhetoric of the repeated 'they want'.

Manifestos – the British Conservative and Labour Parties

A convention of British politics is that the large parties begin their campaigns by issuing a manifesto, a document which 'makes clear', as in the word 'manifest'. This is a written document which sets out their policies in detail in booklet form. These booklets are glossy publications, available for the public to buy or read in libraries, but not usually distributed free to households. The manifesto therefore has a limited readership, although its contents are often referred to by journalists during the campaign, and by opponents afterwards, if they wish to claim that a manifesto 'promise' has been broken. The manifesto is written by a team of writers and is meant to give the views of the party as a whole; increasingly, though, its contents are associated with the leader of the party. This reflects the fact that although British political power is decided by the number of seats won by candidates in constituencies, the campaigning is more akin to the American system where party leaders compete to be president.

In the 1997 General Election in Britain, the two main rivals were the Conservative Party, which had been in power for 18 years, and the Labour Party. Each party's manifesto has a picture of its leader on the front cover, and begins with a foreword from the leader, also accompanied by another picture of him. This foreword is said to come directly from the leaders - the Labour Party claimed that their manifesto was written by Tony Blair with a fountain pen in his garden - although it may well have been written for them by a team of writers. Extracts from each are printed below, with an activity section and a commentary. In each case the focus is to see how persuasive language is used, given that each writer is in a different position: one has power and wants to keep it, the other seeks power.

Activity

Read the following text. Work out responses to the following task and then, if possible, share them with a partner or partners. When you have discussed your responses, write a short commentary on the text.

Task: Analyse the methods used in this text to persuade its readers, by looking in particular at:

(a) the use of metaphor. Two metaphorical fields — i.e. series of connected metaphors — are especially prominent, one involving the idea of a journey in time, the other of fighting. Track the references through the text and say what they contribute to the persuasive message that is being presented.

(b) the use of pronouns in this text. Which are used frequently, and which are not used at all? Suggest some reasons for this.

(c) language features that are found in political speeches, but which are present here in a written text.

Draw comparisons where appropriate with the Democratic Platform.

Text: Conservative Party manifesto

Foreword

The Conservative administrations elected since 1979 are among the most successful in British peacetime history. A country once the sick man of Europe has become its most successful economy. A country once brought to its knees by over-mighty trade unions now has industrial peace. Abroad, the cold war has been won; at home, the rule of law has been restored. The enterprising virtues of the British people have been liberated from the dead hand of the state. There can be no doubt that we have created a better Britain.

Why, then, do we still need a Conservative Government? Because resting on what we have achieved is not enough. To stand still is to fall back. *Our goal must be for Britain to be the best place in the world to live.*

We have turned around our economic fortunes. We have fewer people out of work and more in work than any other major European economy. British people now have the opportunity of a prosperous future. But that prosperity cannot be taken for granted. We have to compete to win. That means a constant fight to keep tight control over public spending and enable Britain to remain the lowest taxed major economy in Europe. It means a continuing fight to keep burdens off business, maintaining our opt-out of the European Social Chapter. If we relax for one moment, our hard won success will slip away again.

The only way to secure this future of opportunity is to stick with the Conservative programme of continuing reform. Now would be the worst possible moment to abandon the pathway to prosperity on which we are set. We must keep up the momentum.

At the same time we must maintain the security that a stable nation provides in an uncertain, fast-changing world. We must protect our constitution and unity as a nation from those who threaten it with unnecessary and dangerous change. And we must stand up for our interests in shaping a free-market Europe of sovereign nation states.

There is, of course, an alternative on offer: to load costs on business while calling it "stakeholding"; to increase the role of the state, while calling it "the community"; to succumb to a centralised Europe while calling it "not being isolated"; to break up our country while calling it "devolution".

To risk this alternative would be a disaster for our country. We have come a very long way. We must be sure that we do not throw away what we have gained, or lose the opportunities we have earned.

You can only be sure with the Conservatives.

Commentary

The usual recipe for political persuasion is to mix praise for your own ideas with criticism of your opponents' record. The Conservatives were in an unusual position in 1997, because they had been in power for so long. This meant that criticism of past regimes would seem to be harking back to a distant past. There is one brief reference to 'over-mighty trade unions' which once brought the country 'to its knees', but no specific date is mentioned. Also, no opponents are actually named, although the paragraph beginning 'There is, of course . . . ' takes some of the Labour Party's key ideas and refers to them as an 'alternative'.

There are two main metaphorical fields used in this text. The first involves the sense of a journey, a journey that has already lasted eighteen years, but a journey which must not cease if the main goal, that Britain is 'the best place in the world to live' is achieved. A similar metaphor was used in the Democratic Party Platform above. This metaphorical field is first identified in the second paragraph: 'resting' is not good enough and 'to stand still is to fall back'. The world is 'fast-moving', so if 'we relax for one moment', success will disappear. 'Now would be the worst possible moment to abandon the pathway . . . We must keep up the momentum.' Risking change of government now would throw away what has been achieved by coming 'a very long way'.

This metaphor of a long journey, of keeping up with a fast-moving world, is temporarily abandoned in the paragraph beginning 'At the same time . . . '. This phrase suggests a change of argument, a switch of emphasis. The world goes on being 'fast-changing', but at this hectic speed we also need the option to be static or 'stable'. As far as Britain's identity as a nation in Europe goes, change becomes threatening if it is 'unnecessary and dangerous'. This contradiction of what has already been said about the need for progress highlights the difficulty the Conservative Party faced over its policy on Europe in 1997. Because the party was itself divided in its attitude towards Europe, a form of words was needed which would not alienate either side: a manifesto is part of a process aimed at winning votes, not losing them.

The idea of 'standing up' to those 'who threaten' is part of the second metaphorical field at work in this text. This involves the idea of fighting, both in terms of the sport of boxing and also full-scale wars. So a country once 'brought to its knees' now holds its place in a 'tougher' world. 'We have to compete to win', which involves a 'constant fight' and a 'continuing fight'.

The first two paragraphs refer to 'Britain'/'British' four times, and to the 'country' twice. Politicians like to invoke a sense of national cohesion, with them at the centre, and this is particularly stressed in this text by the use of pronouns. The dominant words are 'we'/'our'. Even though the text is accompanied by a picture of John Major, and is signed by him at the end, at no time does he refer specifically to himself as 'I'. It was noted in Unit 3 that when politicians use the plural forms of 'we', that this can aim to show that the politician is in touch with all of the country, that they are one of us. This seems to be the intention here, with a deliberate ambiguity surrounding the word 'we' at a number of points. The same effect was noted in the Democratic Platform.

In the third paragraph, for instance, the reference of the word 'we' seems to shift subtly at many different points. In 'We have turned around our economic fortunes', the 'we' refers to the Conservatives, the 'our' to the whole country. In 'We have fewer people out of work . . . ', 'we' refers both to the Conservatives because of what they have done to help, and to the people themselves. 'We have to compete to win' could refer to the Conservatives in the election, but more strongly refers to the people as a whole. The final sentence again seems to carry double possibilities: both the Conservatives and the people have had 'hard won success'. This merging of reference to the party and to the people is of course a deliberate ploy, and it makes the most of the fact that the Conservatives have been in power so long. If the voters feel part of the process, then they will accept the message.

In the final single sentence paragraph, the pronoun 'you' is used. This pronoun too is fluid in its reference: it can be seen as a direct address to the reader, or as a broader reference to everyone as a whole. The final sentence became a slogan of the party during the election and is repeated as a logo on every page of the manifesto. It does not directly urge you to vote Conservative, although that is clearly its purpose, and it too carries some ambiguity.

Many of the features already described here – the use of metaphor, a system of pronouns – have already been seen in Unit 3, which analyses political speeches. Other features which you may have noticed include: the use of repetition ('A country once'); contrasting pairs ('Abroad'/'at home'); rhetorical questions ('Why, then, do we still need a Conservative Government?'); and a significant number of simple one-clause sentences. Although this text is printed in a manifesto, it has many echoes of a speech, perhaps because the public is much more used to hearing politicians than it is to reading their views. Because of this, the manifesto aims to persuade by using some methods that are familiar to the audience. Many similar features were also found in the Democratic Platform.

Activity

Now read the opening section of the Labour Party manifesto on p. 84, which begins with a slogan 'Britain will be better with new Labour.' This is followed by Tony Blair's signature. Alongside both is a picture of Blair. The text forms the first part of a longer introduction to the party's manifesto.

Analyse the methods used in this text to persuade its readers, by looking in particular at:

(a)   the use of metaphor.

(b)   the use of pronouns in this text. Which are used frequently, and which are not used at all? Suggest some reasons for this.

(c)   language features that are found in political speeches, but which are present here in a written text.

Draw comparisons where appropriate with the Conservative manifesto and the Democratic Platform.

Text: Labour Party manifesto

Britain will be better with new Labour

I believe in Britain. It is a great country with a great history. The British people are a great people. But I believe Britain can and must be better: better schools, better hospitals, better ways of tackling crime, of building a modern welfare state, of equipping ourselves for a new world economy.

I want a Britain that is one nation, with shared values and purpose, where merit comes before privilege, run for the many not the few, strong and sure of itself at home and abroad.

I want a Britain that does not shuffle into the new millennium afraid of the future, but strides into it with confidence.

I want to renew our country's faith in the ability of its government and politics to deliver this new Britain. I want to do it by making a limited set of important promises and achieving them. This is the purpose of the bond of trust I set out at the end of this introduction, in which ten specific commitments are put before you. Hold us to them. They are our covenant with you.

I want to renew faith in politics by being honest about the last 18 years. Some things the Conservatives got right. We will not change them. It is where they got things wrong that we will make change. We have no intention or desire to replace one set of dogmas by another.

I want to renew faith in politics through a government that will govern in the interest of the many, the broad majority of people who work hard, play by the rules, pay their dues and feel let down by a political system that gives the breaks to the few, to an elite at the top increasingly out of touch with the rest of us.

And I want, above all, to govern in a way that brings our country together, that unites our nation in facing the tough and dangerous challenges of the new economy and changed society in which we must live. I want a Britain which we all feel part of, in whose future we all have a stake. in which what I want for my own children I want for yours.

In putting the slogan first, followed by Blair's signature and his picture alongside, the Labour manifesto makes a more obvious attempt to create an image at the start of its manifesto. It is clearly using its leader as part of the sell. The party had for some time called itself 'New' Labour in an attempt to reshape its image; this process of adding to the original party name is identical to the way the Democratic Party added the word 'today's' to its name. 'Britain' and 'better', creating an **alliterative** effect, are placed together for the first time. Because Labour had been out of power it could use the comparative 'better' to suggest change for the good. It is much harder for the party in power to talk of change for the better, because this suggests it has failed so far. The Conservatives and Democrats tackled this problem by using the metaphor of a journey that is underway but not finished: indeed, the Conservatives end their opening paragraph by saying that they have already created 'a better Britain'.

In the main body of the text there is the immediate pronoun 'I', a word which John Major did not use throughout his foreword. The use of the first person pronoun confirms the sense that Blair himself is going to be central to the appeal of the party. Each paragraph that follows also begins with this pronoun, forming part of a text which is very strong in its sense of repetition and patterns.

The opening paragraph begins with a simple, short sentence 'I believe in Britain.' This continues the alliterative sound of the slogan, and introduces early the name of the country: both parties make a play for patriotism by frequently mentioning the country and its people in their initial comments. The verb 'believe in' carries a connotation of religious faith, and this idea of 'faith' is developed later in the text. Blair believes in Britain because it is 'great' (also a play upon Great Britain perhaps) – 'great' is mentioned three times. But to be great is not enough; using modal forms Blair insists that Britain 'can and must be better'. 'Better' is then itself repeated three times, and this repetition gives a strong sense that this is a text which also has many similarities to a speech. Each succeeding paragraph begins with 'I want', which is designed to give an escalating emphasis with each use. The second paragraph also contains contrasting pairs in 'merit'/'privilege' and 'many'/'few'.

Various metaphors appear in this text, with an interesting echo at one point of the Conservatives' use of the long journey. Using a very similar idea, Blair does not want Britain to 'shuffle' into the new millennium, he wants it to '[stride] with confidence'. The central metaphor that gives the text its cohesion, though, has been signalled at the very start with the words 'I believe'. This metaphor involves references to do with

Christian religious faith, especially faith in something new, the promise of something better to come in a new life, led by a Messiah figure.

These references are especially numerous, as might be expected, in those paragraphs that begin with the idea of renewed faith. Blair promises a 'bond of trust' based on 'ten commitments', which sounds very similar to the ten commandments. He orders the reader to 'hold us to them' because 'They are our covenant with you', a covenant originally being a promise from God to his people. In being honest, Blair will not replace 'one set of dogmas by another'; instead he will reward the majority who 'play by the rules', a metaphor which may at first sight seem to come from sport, but in this context also evokes a sense of moral commandments.

The Conservative manifesto used 'we' as its dominant pronoun but here there is more variety of pronoun reference. The use of the first person 'I' has already been commented on, and the text also shows the double reference to 'we'/'our'. At times this refers to the whole nation, as in 'our country's faith', at other times it refers to the Labour Party, as in 'We will not change them.'

There are two points in the text, however, where the reader is directly addressed. The first comes at the point where reference is made to 'commitments', which are made to 'you'. The second comes at the end of this extract. In terms of **syntax** this is an unusually complex sentence, with three clauses, the last of which is rather clumsy. This is because of the desire to place emphasis on the word 'want'. Politicians like to sell themselves as family people, and here Blair refers to his own children and his desires for their future. What he wants for his children, he also wants for 'yours'. This is a direct address to the reader, with the reader constructed as someone who has young children.

The three texts used here are extracts from longer texts, which are themselves introductions to documents which give detailed descriptions of party policies. They are persuasive in purpose and have many features of a political speech. None actually says 'vote for us', because they are introducing much fuller documents, but the implication behind each is that once you have read the full manifesto, you will have no alternative but to vote for that party. Whether they succeed in this aim depends not just on how effective their language is; the political views and beliefs that each reader brings to the text will be crucial in deciding whether the persuasion works as far as that reader is concerned.

Local campaigns

The party manifestos are national documents, but political texts are also generated at a local level. A general election in Britain is in fact a series of over 600 separate contests, as the government is formed not necessarily by the party with the most votes overall, but by the party with the most seats. Over many elections the so-called third party of British politics, the Liberal Party, now the Liberal Democrats, gained a much higher proportion of votes than they did seats in parliament. By the time of the 1997 election they had worked out a means of at least partially redressing this imbalance within the first-past-the-post system in Britain. This involved targeting most of their resources on winnable seats, and persuading supporters of other parties to vote tactically in an effort to defeat the party currently in power.

Two such constituencies were Taunton, a rural seat in Somerset, south-west England held by the Conservatives, and Sheffield Hallam, an urban seat in industrial south Yorkshire also held by the Conservatives. Voters in these two areas received a large amount of election material, and were also targeted for visits by leading party figures. Another strategy used by the Liberal Democrats was to produce a simulated newspaper produced in each constituency: the *Somerset Mail* and the *Sheffield Hallam News*. Part of each front page is printed below – it formed the bottom half of the page below a picture featuring the Liberal Democrat candidate.

Activity

Make notes on the following questions:

1   Both texts come from Liberal Democrat party mail-shots, but they appear to be local newspapers. What are the main presentational and linguistic features of newspapers that have been copied here?

2   Although apparently local newspapers, produced in their own areas, the two texts have many similarities in what they are saying and how they say it. What are these similarities, and what does this tell you about who has written the texts?

Text: Somerset Mail

LOOKING GOOD

We're on the brink of success but every vote will be vital,' says Jackie Ballard

With just a few days to go, the Liberal Democrats look to be on the brink of victory in Taunton Constituency. Former Conservative voters, stung by VAT on fuel and worried about the future of schools and the NHS, have decided to vote to back Paddy Ashdown's Liberal Democrats - the clear challengers to the Conservatives in this seat.

Liberal Democrat Candidate Jackie Ballard has offered an attractive and positive alternative on issues like extra funding for the NHS, more resources for education and more police on the beat. It is also clear that her party is expecting a good result. Paddy Ashdown has visited the seat twice during the campaign, when he met local people at Taunton market, talked to a group of first time voters and met workers at Avimo.

Jackie is not taking anything for granted: "I think we have really got our key messages home about who is best placed to beat the Conservative, but with less than a three per cent swing needed, it is vital people go to vote on May 1st.

Former Labour supporters hold the key

Labour supporters may hold the key to the election in this seat. The Conservative's only hope now is that enough people vote Labour to split the vote against him. Many Labour supporters have already taken this message on board. Jackie says "I have also met many people who previously voted Labour, but are now voting for me as they believe the Liberal Democrats have shown a stronger commitment to vital public services than Labour have'.

The result last time	
CON	29,576
LIB DEM	26,240
LAB	8,151

Text: Sheffield Hallam News

PHOTO FINISH

IT'S SO CLOSE!

By Garry White

WITH just a few days to go, Liberal Democrat Richard Allan looks set to overturn the small Conservative majority in **Sheffield Hallam, in another closely fought election contest.**

Former Conservative supporters are angry that the Government broke all their main promises after the last General Election.

Twenty-two tax rises, including VAT on fuel, have left former Conservatives feeling betrayed.

Conservative supporters betrayed

Fears about the future funding of local schools and hospitals have helped drive local voters into the arms of Paddy Ashdown's Liberal Democrats - the clear challengers to the Conservatives in this seat.

Richard Allan is widely credited with having fought a positive campaign based on investing in education, protecting the NHS, putting more police on the beat and looking after our environment.

Unlike the other parties, the Liberal Democrats have said where the money will come from for their proposals.

It's a two horse race in Sheffield Hallam

The votes last time show that Labour cannot win in the Sheffield Hallam constituency

CON 24,693

LIB DEM 17,952

LAB 10,930

The Lib Dems are close to winning

Labour supporters hold the key

With a close finish forecast, Labour supporters may hold the key to the election locally. The Conservatives hope people will vote Labour - because Labour cannot win.

But if enough Labour supporters switch to the Liberal Democrats, the Conservatives will be defeated. Only 6,741 votes separated the Liberal Democrats and the Conservatives last time, whilst Labour trailed a distant third, almost 14,000 votes behind.

—— see back page ——

Commentary

There are a number of graphological features which suggest that these are 'real' newspapers, although they are rather more numerous in the Hallam version. In the *Sheffield Hallam News*, for example, there is the use of large headlines in block capitals, other headlines in lower case letters, different font sizes, highlighted text, the division of the pages into columns, the placing of text in boxes, the attribution of the 'story' to a journalist, the use of sub-headings, the advertising of a story later in the paper, the presentation of statistics in bar chart form. The *Somerset Mail* uses some of these devices, but not all.

There are many similarities in the language and content of the two texts: at some points actual words and phrases are repeated, at others they present very similar ideas. The most important likeness is that both texts are written as though they are stories by journalists; the Hallam version actually names the 'author' of the article, although it is highly likely, given that there are so many similarities to the Somerset version, that this is a fictional name. The advantage of this process is that it presents opinion – which would normally involve using a first-person pronoun as in 'we think . . .' – as fact. So 'Jackie Ballard has offered an attractive and positive alternative' and 'Richard Allen is widely credited with having fought a positive campaign.' The two candidates do not speak for themselves (unless quoted) but are spoken about.

The opening of each story begins with the same words – 'With just a few days to go' – and thereafter there are direct repetitions ('Labour supporters hold the key'/'more police on the beat') and close echoes ('the result last time'/'the votes last time'). Tax rises, the NHS, and re-sources for education are among the political issues that are repeated and each story contains a reference to the national leader, Paddy Ashdown, as well as the local candidate. The way such specific details are repeated suggests that these are not locally produced 'newspapers', but are part of the national campaign devised and written centrally by the party.

The purpose of these 'newspapers' is to persuade people to vote Liberal Democrat, and they use a number of strategies which highlight their role as the 'third' party. Whereas the two big parties rarely concede that their opponents have any supporters at all, the Lib Dems are happy to concede that not all voters are inevitably on their side. Conservative supporters, we are told, have now lost their allegiance and have become 'Former Conservatives' – and so will vote Lib Dem this time. The case is different with Labour supporters though; they have not changed their view, it's just that they can't actually win, so it makes sense for them to vote tactically for the Lib Dems too. The bar charts, with their not-quite-to-scale images, reinforce the point that it's 'a two horse race'. The Lib Dems also stress the closeness of the campaigns: they want people to feel that their vote will be significant to the result, because then they are more likely actually to vote.

Finally, it is worth looking at how this text constructs its overall persuasive message. It has already been mentioned above that each text has a real writer, or writers (the party's central campaign managers) and an implied writer (the local journalist – who in one example is actually given a name). Readership also works on two levels. The implied readers are constructed by the text as voters sitting at home with their local paper, making up their mind how to vote. The real readers, though, know all along that this is an election communication from a political party that is trying to woo them. The real writers and real readers are engaged in a fictional relationship created by the text.

Both Jackie Ballard and Richard Allen were elected to Parliament in the 1997 election.

Reporting the results

The 1997 campaign saw a huge victory for New Labour. In the words of the conventional, if rather strange metaphor, given that it literally refers to an environmental disaster, it was 'a landslide'. Not all the results were available when British newspapers were printed on the morning of May 2nd 1997, but the headlines vied with each other to describe the enormity of what had happened. The two units on campaigning are rounded off with a look at some of these headlines and the paragraphs that followed.

Unit 2 explored some ideas around metaphor and transitivity. Transitivity involves looking at the language used to describe:

◎ what happens;
◎ who the participants are (both those who do something and those affected by what is done);
◎ what the circumstances are.

Blame or credit can be attributed, for instance, by either emphasising the role of a participant or by minimising it. This process can include the naming labels given to the participant as well as the grammatical foregrounding or backgrounding of their role.

In the case of the election results of 1997, there were a number of possible ways in which they could be presented by newspapers as the results came out. It has been noted earlier that British elections are increasingly seen as presidential-style contests – that the main battle is between party leaders. This suggests that news stories could focus on either (a) Blair's Labour victory, (b) Major's Conservative defeat, or (c) both. Naming labels for the key players would be important, as would the metaphorical language used to describe what had happened.

Some of the issues worth exploring in these texts are as follows:

◎ Who is foregrounded, the winners or the losers?
◎ Are winners or losers named individuals, are their parties named, or both?
◎ What naming labels are used to describe leaders?
◎ What metaphors are used to describe what has happened, and what is their effect on the reader?
◎ What attitudes to the result are expressed by the newspapers, either overtly or implicitly?

Texts: Newspapers, May 2nd 1997

The following is a selection of front-page stories on the day after the election on May 1st 1997. Headlines are in bold print, followed by the opening paragraphs of the articles.

> **YES**
> **BLAIR LANDSLIDE SEALED WITH A X** [alongside picture of Blair and wife]
>
> Triumphant Tony Blair was sweeping to power early today. The Labour leader was set for the most sensational ever election victory...
> (the *Mirror*)

The word 'Yes' echoes the cry of triumph of the sportsplayer or sports fan. The cry of triumph could come from two possible sources, Blair or the *Mirror*, but the most foregrounded point is that the *Mirror* wanted this result to happen. Next to be stressed is Blair's role as leader, with the first reference to his party coming in the second sentence of the article that follows. The pun on 'X', which is both a kiss and a vote, and the prominence of a picture showing husband and wife kissing, again places individuals before party. There is no reference at all to the defeated Conservatives.

YES IT'S ME

160 LEAD AS BLAIR STORMS TO No 10 [alongside picture of Blair reading previous day's the *Sun*, with the visible headline 'It must be you' and the National Lottery logo pointing at him]

Jubilant Tony Blair was heading for 10 Downing Street last night with a MASSIVE majority of around 160 seats. The Labour leader – who read of his destiny in the *Sun* – crushed John Major's tired-out Tories in spectacular style.

(the *Sun*)

This headline also contains a triumphant 'yes', but links it closely with the winning of the National Lottery, which in turn had been part of the paper's coverage the previous day (at that time the National Lottery's main slogan was 'it could be you'). The connection with the lottery is understandable in one way, in that Blair had won the biggest prize of all, but surprising in another, as the election had not in fact been a lottery in the sense of it being the result of casual chance. The *Sun*, however, had a history of featuring lottery stories, so this linked in with its house style.

The *Sun* had urged readers to vote Labour, but for many years previously it had been a staunch supporter of the Conservative Party. In its picture and its article it places itself as part of the story, but it is nonetheless a little more distanced in its support than The *Mirror*. 'Yes it's me' implies that Blair is speaking rather than the *Sun* itself.

'Blair' in the main headline becomes 'Jubilant Tony Blair' in the article, then 'Labour leader'. This time the losers are eventually mentioned in the alliterative phrase 'tired-out Tories'. In calling the Conservatives this, the *Sun* is implying a reason for its changing sides.

In a new variation on the metaphorical field of extreme weather conditions, Blair is said to 'storm' into number 10.

Activity

Following the example of the analysis above, provide similar brief commentaries on the following headlines/openings of articles. With each one comes a description of the accompanying picture and whom the paper supported before the election.

1   **BLAIR'S BRITAIN IS BORN AFTER TORY WIPEOUT** [Text alongside picture of Blair with hands clasped together]
Tony Blair tore home early today to an extraordinary landslide Commons majority, ending 18 years of Conservative rule.
(the *Independent* – usually a Labour/Lib Dem supporter)

2   **MAYDAY MASSACRE** [Picture of Blair with family]
Tony Blair was sweeping into Downing Street early today with what looked like a historic General Election landslide . . . It seemed that a seismic shift in the nation's political mood had condemned the Tories to their heaviest defeat this century.
(the *Daily Mail* – Conservative supporter)

3   **LANDSLIDE**
Tory vote collapses as Labour sweeps in [Picture of Blair giving triumphant wave]
Eighteen years of Tory rule came to an end last night as Tony Blair led the Labour Party back from the political wilderness to a landslide General Election victory.
(*Newcastle Journal* – Labour supporter)

Extension

Written texts that are part of election campaigns provide plenty of scope for research projects, but they need a sharp linguistic focus if they are to be effective. This unit and the previous one have already given some ideas of the sort of texts that can be investigated and the language features to look for.

For each of the categories listed below, it is important to have a clear sense of what you want to cover, and the range of material you want to look at. Comparing the output of different political parties is one obvious way, but it is also possible to specialise in the output of one party or even one politician. Another angle to take is to look at how various parties approach a key political issue, such as education, welfare or economic policy.

If you are able to gain access to material from other countries, this could also lead to interesting research, either by analysing it in its own right, or comparing it with the British model.

The following texts have been looked at in Units 4 and 5:

1   Party slogans.
2   Election posters.
3   Election manifestos.
4   Election leaflets and mail-shots.
5   Newspaper coverage of results.

In addition, other possible areas of research include:

6   Party political broadcasts, on television and/or radio.
7   Campaign speeches by leading figures.
8   Newspaper editorials, especially those just before an election when the paper advises its readers how to vote.
9   Interviews on television and/or radio.
10   Local coverage in various media.

Answering questions

One of the most common accusations levelled at politicians is that they never answer the question. Tony Blair, when Leader of the Opposition in Britain, would often taunt the then Prime Minister John Major by demanding an answer to a question 'Yes or No'. As will be seen in this unit, such simple responses are not always possible.

There are in reality many reasons why politicians might not want to give a yes/no answer, not least because in an age when every comment can be recorded, stored and retrieved for playback at a moment's notice, they are afraid that a straight answer will return to haunt them. The important linguistic point that will be explored in this unit, however, is that the terms 'straight question' and 'straight answer' can be misleading, because they suggest that questioning and answering are essentially straightforward. Unit 2 looked at some of the ways metaphor is used in political language. A commonly used metaphor surrounding questions and answers is that of a journey. So 'straight' or 'direct' questions demand 'straight' or 'direct' answers, which are preferably 'short'. If an answer is going to be a 'long' one, then it helps if we are taken through it 'step by step'. The route must remain direct though: if the respondents 'wander from the point', or 'go off at tangents', then there is every chance they will be 'twisting' their argument or 'deviating from the point'. If they say nothing significant at all, then they are 'going round in circles'. Sometimes in this metaphorical field of reference, the actual mode of transport is suggested: politicians sometimes 'derail' talks (train), create a 'stumbling block' (walking), or 'enter clear waters' (sailing).

The metaphorical straight or simple line of argument referred to in a 'straight question'/'straight answer', then, implies that such questions allow a simple or direct response, without any twists or turns, and that the response can begin with the words 'yes' or 'no'.

It is also worth noting at this point that question-and-answer sessions with politicians, whether in Parliament or on radio or television, carry the expectation that the respondent to the questions will give fairly detailed answers. The 'rules' of this type of question-and-answer speech event allow and expect the respondent to articulate a detailed set of arguments that extend beyond the apparent simplicity of some questions. Although the politicians who respond to questioning are often accused of not answering the question directly, if they did so merely giving yes/no answers, the rules of the speech event would be broken and the politicians would appear unusual, even strange in their responses. Politicians outside the mainstream of party politics have sometimes used this fact to highlight their independence, deliberately breaking the rules by giving brief answers and so suggesting their difference from the rest of the candidates.

Because it is the politicians' answers that are criticised as being evasive, it is usually only the answers that are analysed in any great detail. What is often forgotten in this process, though, is that the question and the answer form a linguistic pair, and that you cannot analyse one, without looking at the other. To begin with, therefore, it is helpful to look at some ideas surrounding the way questions are formed.

Types of question

Questions can be defined as utterances which require information and opinions that the questioner does not know (one exception to this is the test or quiz, where the questioner does know the answer but wants to see if others do). Broadly speaking they can be categorised into three main types:

1   *Yes/no questions,* which permit a simple positive or negative reply and often have the pattern of auxiliary verb followed by the subject, as in 'are you going home now?' A variation on this structure, but one which still permits a yes/no answer, involves the use of a **tag question**, as in 'you are going home now, aren't you?' Tag questions, which involve a positive (here 'you are going home') with a negative ('aren't you?'), or vice versa, contain within them a sense of what the required answer should be. In this case – 'you are going home now, aren't you?' – the expected answer is 'yes'.

2   Questions known as *wh/questions* because they begin with a word that signals a question, such as 'who'/'which'/'where'/'why'/ 'when'/'what' and 'how'. An example is 'why are you going home now?'

3   *Alternative questions*, which always contain the word 'or' and which offer alternative responses as in 'are you going home now or later?'

This general description of types of question looks straightforward, but does not give the full picture: questions can be far more complex than suggested in the outline above, not least because they can themselves contain **presuppositions** and **assertions.** A presupposition is a fact or opinion that is embedded in a question and assumed by the questioner to be already known and agreed. An assertion is a declaration that something is true or right, when this may not necessarily be the case. In these cases, when seeking further information, the questioner has already taken some things for granted. The respondent, on the other hand, may wish to disagree with what has been presupposed or asserted.

One reason why politicians have to be very careful when answering a question is that they cannot allow presuppositions and assertions to go unchallenged if they disagree with them. In challenging them, it may then appear that they are not answering the question. Before looking at the sort of question that politicians are asked, the idea of presuppositions and assertions can be seen in the following example.

The question 'Newcastle United have been playing badly in recent games; did they win yesterday?' looks simple enough: the answer, it would appear must be 'yes' or 'no'. The utterance begins, however, with an assertion, that the team has been playing badly of late in the opinion of the questioner. A simple yes/no answer to the question will appear to confirm the assertion, which may not necessarily be the opinion of the responder. The question also contains a presupposition, that Newcastle actually played a game yesterday; if their game was postponed, you could technically answer 'no', but the questioner might assume they had lost a game that never took place. Another problem with the yes/no answer to this question is that it does not allow for a third eventuality: the match could have been drawn. Although you could again simply answer 'no', which would in one sense be true, it would again be a misleading answer unless you added more information. What this example shows, then, is two important points: that questions often contain assertions and presuppositions that need to be recognised when an answer is analysed, and that not all questions that appear to be of the yes/no type can be reduced to a simple binary formula of 'if not one, then the other': 'yes' or 'no'.

Activity

The following question was put to the Northern Irish politician David Trimble on a radio current affairs programme. At the time there were very delicate negotiations taking place in an attempt to gain peace in Northern Ireland, and a vital deadline was approaching; leaders of what were seen as the two main sides in the talks were interviewed to see if they thought a treaty would be signed. This is a spoken question – the interviewer was in a London studio, Mr Trimble on the phone in Belfast – so it does not have the formal composition that you would expect to find in a written one; the text has been punctuated conventionally to help you when reading. Using the discussion earlier in this unit:

1   Say to which of the three main categories this question belongs, and write out the core part of the question in your own words.
2   List any presuppositions and assertions that are contained in the question.
3   Break down the answer into a series of steps which show clearly the line of argument that is taken.
4   Do you think that the answer to the question is, in effect, yes or no?

Question: But now everyone's got to make a compromise and I'm sure you'd agree on that. It's the extent and nature of the compromises that are the sticking points and your deputy leader has said he doesn't give it more than a 50 per cent chance of success – so are you more optimistic than that?

Answer: Well, as I said, there are still serious difficulties which have to be resolved and we are dealing with a rather unique set of problems, problems which in a normal arrangement wouldn't exist . . . Our opponents want a veto in the assembly. Now this is not a normal way of proceeding. We understand their concerns and are ready to meet their concerns if we can but the problem is how do you do that and still have an institution that's workable.

Commentary

This is a yes/no question, in that it uses the 'are you . . .?' form. The essence of the question is something like 'are you going to agree a treaty with your opponents?', but direct reference to signing an agreement or treaty does not actually appear in the question.

A number of assertions can be seen in the question:

- a compromise is needed for a peace treaty
- both sides have to compromise
- you must agree that compromise is needed
- the type of compromise has not yet been agreed
- the leader's deputy thinks there is only a 50/50 chance of a treaty.

Presuppositions are:

- a compromise is the way to solve the problem
- only if the interviewee thinks there is more than a 50/50 chance can there be a successful treaty.

What this analysis shows is that this is a very complex question, and that the politician cannot, in any meaningful way, answer simply 'yes' or 'no'. Not surprisingly the answer to this question seems, on the surface, to be evasive.

It should be remembered, as with all live interviews, that this is spoken language. Even though the politician will have some idea of the questions to be asked, and may even have asked for them in advance of the interview, the reply is still unscripted and relatively spontaneous. In this case it was also conducted over the telephone, so there was no face-to-face contact with the interviewer. If the answer is broken down into a series of steps, however, it is possible to work out how the answer is given:

- there are still serious difficulties
- these difficulties are unique so there are no previous examples to copy
- our opponents want a veto
- we understand our opponents' concerns up to a point but . . .
- . . . we're not prepared to give them a veto.

In other words, the answer is 'no'. If Mr Trimble had simply said this, however, it would have appeared that he was rejecting all of the assertions about the need for compromise and that he was therefore being extreme and inflexible. Indeed, he goes out of his way to appear flexible by saying that he understands his opponents' concerns, although using the word 'opponent' in itself suggests, perhaps, that he sees the question as one of two sides fighting a metaphorical battle.

Confrontational questions

Listen to archive footage of media interviews with politicians earlier this century and they sound very strange to our ears. The politicians are asked very brief, direct questions and their answers sound wooden enough to suggest that the whole process was rehearsed. But perhaps most striking of all is the deferential way in which the interviewers perform their role: they are extremely polite, they do not interrupt, their questions do not appear to contain assertions or presuppositions. Nowadays the situation is very different, with a much more confrontational style of questioning, conducted by media figures who themselves have a high profile. An analysis of part of one such interview shows the difficulty politicians face when expected to give a straight answer.

Activity

In July 1998, Prime Minister Tony Blair's government announced substantial increases in spending on education and health (see also Unit 2). The following morning he was interviewed on BBC Radio 4 by one of their leading journalists, John Humphrys. The interview took place at 10 Downing Street at peak listening time.

The main topic for the interview was extra money for education and health – to many people a good thing. Because such interviews are now essentially confrontational, however, Humphrys initially concentrated his questions on where the money would come from.

How does the interviewer (JH) frame his questions to Tony Blair (TB), and what challenges does he face in answering them?

The following spoken text has been punctuated conventionally.

JH: But one of your problems, perhaps the biggest problem, is the welfare budget, the welfare bill. You used to say that as we get the welfare bills down, then we'll be able to put more money into education and health and all the rest of it. Well, now you've stopped saying that all of a sudden. You've made assumptions, you haven't got it down, in fact everything you've done has put the welfare bill up, but all of a sudden you're saying now that it was unrealistic - we couldn't ever have done that really, we're just going to carry on anyway.

TB: No. If I can just set out exactly what we said, what we said in our manifesto.

JH: I've got it here in front of me. Shall I help you out? [Quotes from manifesto] But you haven't been doing that.

TB: No, no, hang on, John, that is what we have been doing. It's very very important that people make a clear distinction here, because what you've just read out is precisely what I would say both we should do and are doing.

Commentary

Humphrys' first 'question' is very long, and although interviewers can interrupt answers, it is very unusual for questions to be interrupted. He begins with an assertion, that the government has problems with welfare bills, the presupposition being that with high welfare bills it cannot afford extra money. He then accuses Blair of first saying one thing — reduce welfare spending and there will be money for other things — but of now changing policy. This is followed by the assertion that welfare spending has not been reduced, indeed it has gone up, but the government is carrying on as though it had been reduced.

Humphrys' expression is informal, especially in the way he creates his own version of what Blair 'used to say'. Phrases like 'and all the rest of it', 'all of a sudden you're saying', 'we couldn't ever have done that really' and 'carry on anyway' have the effect of diminishing the significance of Blair's statements, even though he did not actually say them.

One of the problems for Blair here is that there is no formal question asked at all. Although Humphrys finishes with a rising tone on 'carry on anyway', indicating that Blair should speak now, there is no clear reference point for him to approach first.

Blair begins by saying 'no'. This is not in answer to a question, more an attempt to say that he disagrees with the assertions that have been made. He is barely into his reply, which attempts to put the record straight, before he is interrupted with a verbatim reading of his own words from a previous source. Although it is suggested that this reading of the manifesto will 'help him out', it is in fact a further challenge: the last thing Blair wants at this point is for his exact words to heard by the audience. This interruption ends with another assertion, with no explicit form of question, although the tag 'have you?' is implied at the end of 'but you haven't been doing that.'

Blair again says 'no' in an attempt to deny the assertion of broken promises, and in saying 'hang on' he is asking for time to give a full answer. He then begins to counter Humphrys' various assertions by saying that he is doing what the manifesto promised – and 'people', the listeners, must understand this.

This exchange is typical of the questioning faced by leading politicians. There is no doubt that Humphrys has a clear grasp of the detail involved in this issue, and that he is not overawed by Blair's position. Blair himself seems to accept the questioning, although to object to it would make him appear weak and suspicious. The confrontational style, however, even if it shows that politicians are answerable to the people, does not in itself allow politicians to explain policy; instead they are constantly attempting to deny presuppositions and assertions made by the interviewer. The way the questions are framed, often without any central focal point, also shows how difficult it can be for politicians, at least sometimes, to give a straight answer.

Activity

In the light of the analysis above, write your own commentary on the following exchange which came towards the end of the interview quoted above. 'Croneyism', referred to in the question, was a name given by journalists to the accusation that the government was allowing favoured people private meetings with important ministers. No commentary accompanies this text.

> JH: You said to the nation as a whole 'look, trust me. You can trust me.' You since talked about having to be seen as purer than pure. Does it worry you that the trust factor, according to the latest opinion polls and according to lots of other people, that the trust factor in your government has suffered and perhaps you personally have suffered as a result of what is now being described as croneyism?
>
> TB: Well, it certainly shouldn't, I mean –
>
> JH: (interruption) What, shouldn't worry you?
>
> TB: No. I mean of course I'm always concerned if people make allegations that the government is in some way doing something dishonest, and anything of that nature we'll investigate.

Parliamentary Question Time

The discussion on questions and answers has so far concentrated on the media interview, where politicians are faced by professional interviewers who would claim to be impartial – in other words they belong to no particular side themselves but are seeking information for the public. The work already done in this unit on assertion and presupposition shows that things are rather more complex than this, and that politicians are often asked complex questions that cannot be answered in the simple way that is often expected of them. The idea of the impartial questioner does not arise, however, when politicians are asked questions by other politicians in their parliaments or equivalent institutions. Here the position is much clearer: the questioner will be either friend or foe, and the sort of question asked will clearly reflect this fact. Prime Minister's Questions in the British House of Commons provides useful data for analysing this process.

Prime Minister's Questions takes place once a week when Parliament is sitting. For half an hour the Prime Minister is asked a range of questions by Members of Parliament, including several from the Leader of the Opposition. It is argued by those who make large democratic claims for Parliament that this session shows democracy at its best, where the most important politician in the land is called to account by the people's representatives. When these sessions are studied closely, however, it becomes clear that this process is not as productive as is claimed.

The questions that the Prime Minister is asked come from one of two groups – either their own supporters, or members of all the opposition parties. Questions from their own side will usually be known in advance, and sometimes even 'planted', giving the PM a chance to make a speech on a favoured topic, rather than a reply to a challenging question. The Opposition, on the other hand, will be trying to ask difficult questions in an attempt to catch out the PM. The PM, though, will have had an army of researchers working at questions that might be asked, so that there will be information at hand.

What this all means is that the reality of Prime Minister's questions is rather different from the claims made for it on behalf of open democracy. It is in many ways a performance: an opportunity to give speeches on favoured topics, and a show of strength against tricky opponents. The idea of politics as a game or a war is again evident – it is the PM's survival under fire, an ability to deal with the flak, that is often the main issue, not a sophisticated working out of policy. Reporting of the event nearly always talks in terms of a victory for either the PM, or the Opposition leader, and broadcast media concentrate on soundbites that are about confrontation rather than explanation. The event is often very rowdy, with frequent interruptions, adding to the impression of a battle rather than a calm debate.

The idea of survival under political fire relies upon a number of factors, but one is at the heart of the process: in the linguistic conventions of political questions and answers, there is no place for silence, for doubt or reflection. Winners talk - they talk with as much certainty as they can muster, and shoot down as many opponents as they can. It is no accident that Prime Ministers are often judged by the media on their 'performance' at question time, rather than for the quality of their comments.

A typical opposition question is one that accuses the ruling party of corruption. Conventions of address in Parliament are retained in these examples. Prime Minister Tony Blair was asked:

> When will the right honourable gentleman live up to his promise of rooting out corruption in local government…? Is it not obvious, even to him, that Labour councils are riven with dissent and rotten to the core?

He replied:

> Every time there have been allegations of corruption in Labour councils, we have investigated them, in stark contrast to a Conservative party, which allowed corruption and wrongdoing to carry on and for years did nothing - but that is the difference between Conservative and Labour values.

In simple terms, the question comes in two parts: a wh/question, followed by a yes/no question. The first part, though, is not really asking the question 'when?' with the expectation that he will reply 'next Tuesday'. The presupposition carried by the question is that he will never keep the promises that he makes. The second part is in the form of a tag question, and as has been seen earlier in this unit, tag questions carry a sense of what the answer should be. 'Is it not obvious' is a formal way of saying 'isn't it obvious' and the expected answer is therefore 'yes'. But it is unlikely that Tony Blair will admit to leading a party 'riven with dissent and rotten to the core'. So in effect neither part of the question is really there to be answered; it is instead a challenge to the PM to see if he can reply in a similarly aggressive way.

This is compounded by the aside 'even to him', which in its ambiguity carries a number of possible meanings – is Blair too stupid to see the obvious, or too cunning to intervene in corruption? When insults cannot be openly traded, as they cannot be in the British Parliament, then they have to be implied. The pronoun 'him', rather than 'you', is a product of the rules of parliamentary address, which say that speakers must refer to other members of the house in the impersonal third person; it also allows the implied insult to be less obvious, but nonetheless still noticeable.

Blair has not really been asked a question that he can be expected to answer, and he does not do so. Instead he picks up on the broad topic of the question – corruption – and says in effect two things:

1   Labour always investigates allegations, with the implication that it often finds nothing wrong.
2   The Conservatives allowed actual corruption to flourish and they never did anything about it at all.

He ends with a statement, designed to bring cheers from his own side, that his party has superior values to the Opposition's. In effect, then, question and answer has really been an exchange of insults – 'you're corrupt', followed by 'no we're not, you are!'

Questions from the Prime Minister's own side usually serve two main functions: to introduce pre-arranged topics which the PM may wish to speak about, and to encourage attacks on opponents. Typical examples of this process are:

1   'Does my right hon. friend agree that the Conservative opposition to a minimum wage is wrong morally and economically and that his policies have the support of the vast majority of people?'
2   'Will my right honourable friend treat with the contempt that it deserves this pathetic apology for an opposition, who do not deal with crime, jobs, welfare and all the issues about which people care?'
3   'Will the Prime Minister accept that the Budget was magnificent?'

Not surprisingly, questions such as these are much more likely to receive 'yes' as an answer. They also go largely unreported because of their uncontroversial nature.

Activity

The following, slightly edited exchange took place in the British Parliament when Prime Minister Tony Blair was questioned by the Leader of the Opposition, William Hague.

1   Using the analysis of questions and answers discussed in this unit, write a commentary on the language used by each politician, including the way each of them uses statistical data to reinforce their points.

2   Although this is technically a question-and-answer session, it can be argued that both politicians make speeches. Referring to information about speeches in Unit 3, what typical features of speech-making can be seen here?

3   To reinforce work done on metaphor in Unit 2, what examples of metaphor are used in Hague's last question and Blair's last answer?

4   It was stated earlier that the purpose of questions is to gather information and opinions that are not known by the questioner. To what extent, do you think, does that process happen here?

Text : Parliamentary Question Time

Hague: Has the Prime Minister seen the figures showing that over the 18 years of Conservative government national health service spending rose by 3 per cent a year and that next year it will rise by 2.2 per cent? Are those figures correct?

Blair: The figures indeed show that to be the case over 18 years, but in the last 2 years national health spending rose in real terms by less than 2 per cent. This government have considerably improved on that.

Hague: The truth then is that this government are not matching the previous government's performance. Will he acknowledge that the increase in spending is now less than it was under Conservative governments over those 18 years?

Blair: No. I certainly will not agree with that as it is plainly wrong. First we are putting far more money into the NHS - now more than 1.7 billion - than was proposed by the Conservatives. Secondly, we are spending far more - more than £300 million - than the Conservatives were due to spend. The right honourable gentleman is wrong on every count.

Hague: The Prime Minister's answer bears no resemblance to truth. He promised the British people so much on health: he promised to reduce waiting lists, but they are now bigger; he promised to increase spending on the NHS, but the government have cut growth in spending; and he promised to keep open specific hospitals, but his government has been busy closing them. Is that not a step-by-step betrayal of the NHS?

Blair: What a cheek, honestly. We are spending more money, far more money, than the Conservatives would have spent. The British people know perfectly well that the Conservative government did everything it could to undermine the national health service. We will put the national health service back on its feet, as we promised.

(Hansard: 1 April 1998)

Commentary

Politicians frequently use statistical data to support their arguments, making sure that they choose the best interpretation — or spin — to suit their cause. Here it is clear that Hague intends to quote figures that cover

18 years, while Blair is only going to look at the last 2 years of Conservative rule. There is already, in the opening exchanges, an inevitability that neither will be prepared to change their spin on these figures, and that the only issue really at stake is who can score more points from his opponent.

Hague asks two questions in his first 'go'. Both are yes/no questions, but they are clearly the opening part of the real question that is to follow. He is at this point seeing how Blair will react to the trap he is setting.

Blair, without quite saying 'yes', concedes that the figures exist, but before he is asked another question, he puts his own spin on them by making a positive reading for his side from them. In this way he anticipates the question that he knows is coming.

Hague then asserts that there is only one truthful way to look at the figures − his way − and asks the yes/no question that was implied in his first contribution: will Blair accept that the government is not increasing spending in the way the Conservatives did? Blair replies 'no', and asserts that Hague's reading of the figures is wrong. Instead of referring back to the original percentages, he this time adds statistics of his own, quoting two large sums of money, which sound impressive but have little real meaning in this context. He repeats the accusation that Hague is 'wrong', giving more emphasis by adding 'on every count', even though it is he who has counted by saying 'first' and 'secondly'.

In his final contribution Hague once more refers to truth, or lack of it. In effect he then makes a speech, adding a question, of sorts, at the end. Having introduced the idea of a promise made to the British people, he then uses a three-part list, each part containing the repeated words 'he promised'. Each of the three parts also contains a contrastive pair: 'reduce'/'bigger'; 'increase'/'cut'; 'open'/'closing'. These contrasting words are all about relative amount, highlighting the central point about spending that Hague has been making from the start.

Hague's question, when it arrives, contains an example of metaphor and metonymy; there is a metaphorical journey represented by 'step-by-step', while the NHS metonymically stands for the patients that are betrayed by government policy. It could be argued here that the metonymic reference to the institution − the NHS − rather than to the actual patients, weakens the strength of the question.

Because of the convention of question and answer sessions, Blair is in the fortunate position of knowing that he will always have the last word. This time he does not answer the question, but instead ridicules his opponent. He then echoes much of the language that was central to Hague's speech − he too refers to the British people, not in terms of their receiving broken promises, but that they know the real truth. He accuses the Conservatives of undermining the health service – the word 'under-mine' relates to war, the tactic of digging tunnels under a building and then blowing it up. He ends in the way he started, saying his government are spending more than the previous one and using, perhaps uncon-sciously, a metaphor of health improvement when he talks of the health service being put 'back on its feet'. The health service itself becomes a patient, about to be brought back to good health by his government.

Although there is much political rhetoric here, there is no real discussion of issues. No one has shifted their position, no one has pro-duced extended arguments about the need for a health service, there has been no real discussion of the issues involved. It would appear from the linguistic analysis above that the claims made for Prime Minister's Questions – that it shows open democracy working at its best – are misplaced. Instead, it seems to be much more about political point scoring.

The same point was made by the independent Member of Parlia-ment and former journalist, Martin Bell. He asked the Prime Minister whether 'members might ask the questions they wish to ask rather than those they have been encouraged or instructed by others to ask. Would this not be to everyone's benefit, including his own?' The reply did not answer the question.

Cheats and liars

Earlier in this unit it was noted that the British Parliament has rules of procedure that govern the language that is used in a whole range of contexts. For example, members have to be addressed with formal titles, such as their job if they are a minister (i.e. 'Would the Foreign Secretary agree ...'), or their constituency ('Does the Honourable Member for Exeter think that ...'). In addition, they must be referred to in the third person - 'he'/'she' rather than 'you'. This formality is designed to take out all sense of personality in debate, to make the ideas more important than the people. As part of the same process, there are strict rules governing what members are allowed to call their opponents: they cannot be called liars or cheats; they cannot be accused of being drunk; they cannot be imitated or physically mocked.

This does not mean that members are perpetually respectful to each other - they have to find less direct means of being hostile to their opponents. Some examples from 1998 include:

I have now remembered the pedigree of the honourable gentleman.

It is a bit of an own goal to say the opposite of what your colleague said.

The Prime Minister's answer bore so little resemblance to the truth ...

That was an interesting question, but it was not truthful and not worth answering.

In the last two examples quoted, members were allowed to deny the truth of what opponents said, but they did not go so far as to call them liars. If Members of Parliament do, in the judgement of the Speaker, overstep the bounds of conventional language, they are forced to 'withdraw' a remark – to unsay it. In most cases they do withdraw, although this in one sense merely reinforces what they have said in the first place, especially when the withdrawal itself repeats the accusation in more polite terms. Some MPs will deliberately break the rules, knowing that convention allows them to withdraw later.

The Australian House of Representatives has many similar rules to the British Parliament, and in its *Rules Governing Content of Speeches* it outlaws 'offensive or disorderly words' and 'references to, and reflections on, members'. Nonetheless, it has a tradition of its members being less constrained by rules of formality than its British counterpart. One speaker who became renowned for his 'colourful language' (as it was officially described in parliamentary records) was Prime Minister Paul Keating.

In the 1980s and 1990s he described the Opposition in the following terms:

They are basically a bunch of tax cheats.

They are the thugs of Australian politics. They are the constitutional vandals of Australia.

You were heard in silence, so some of you scumbags ... should wait until you hear the response from me.

They are lice.

Individual members were addressed as follows:

He is brain-damaged.

The honourable member is a member with a criminal intellect, and is a criminal in my view.

This piece of vermin.

He is simply a shiver looking for a spine to run up.

The honourable member is a loopy crim . . . a stupid foul-mouthed grub . . . a piece of criminal garbage.

The mixture of formal procedural language ('the honourable member is . . .') with informal abuse ('. . . a stupid foul-mouthed grub') creates a particularly interesting effect, one which Keating was no doubt consciously cultivating as part of his political image. Even though he had to 'withdraw' many of these comments, he had already made his point.

Activity

The following statements were made in the Australian House of Representatives in 1998; all of them were required to be withdrawn by the Speaker of the House.

You fool

Traitor

Maybe even you understand that

Conspirator extraordinaire

You are an idiot

Are you sober enough tonight

It is deceitful

You fraud

You're a ventriloquist's dummy

You were making racist comments

Looking like a thug, sounding like a thug and, without doubt, being a thug

You are a disgrace

The dope sitting next to you

Tell another lie

Phony muckraker

You're a liar

He has broken his word

Akin to treason

For each of these statements, say why you think it was required to be withdrawn. Then, using this data, compile a brief set of rules, outlining what members are not allowed to say about each other.

Summary

There is a widely held assumption that politicians never answer questions directly, and that they have various formulaic strategies for avoiding giving a straight answer to a straight question. As has been seen in this unit, though, the commonly held view of evasiveness is an over-simple one. Politicians are rarely asked simple questions in media interviews, so to expect a yes/no reply can sometimes be unreasonable. When they question each other in parliament, on the other hand, they are working within the conventions of a system of party politics that often places formalised confrontation ahead of genuine information and point-of-view.

Extension

1   The final part of this unit refers to some of the conventions of parliamentary language, and the ways in which politicians can attack their opponents. There is considerable scope in both areas for further research, which could include:

- a more detailed look at the speech conventions in parliament(s)
- comparison of formal language use in different parliamentary systems
- the language of political attack, either in parliaments, outside or both.

With many parliaments and assemblies now placing their proceedings on the Internet, data should be relatively easy to find.

2   This unit has concentrated on questions and answers as seen in parliament and in media interviews. There is considerable scope in both areas for further research, with data readily available from parliamentary broadcasts, regular current affairs programmes and the Internet. Comparing answers given by rival politicians to the same questions can be a useful focus, especially at times of leadership contests or when politicians agree to meet each other in face-to-face broadcasts. Radio phone-ins with leading politicians also offer the opportunity to analyse the way politicians reply to questions put by the general public.

index of terms

This is a form of combined glossary and index. Listed below are some of the key terms used in the book, together with brief definitions for purposes of reference. The page references will normally take you to the first use of the term in the book, where it will be shown in bold.

active (see **voice**)

adverbial 24
This is used to describe words, clauses, or phrases which act as adverbs. This means that they add detail and specificity to a verb, often in terms of how, where or when, i.e. 'they played *well*', 'they played *on an old rubbish tip*', 'they played *yesterday*'.

agent (see **voice**)

alliteration 85
A series of words beginning with the same sound.

analogy 27
A comparison between one thing and another, in an attempt to explain or clarify a certain situation.

anaphoric reference 25
This points backwards in a text to something that has already been mentioned. For example, 'The President denied allegations of wrongdoing, saying that *they* are complete lies.' Here 'they' refers back to 'allegations'.

aspect 62
This is to do with the way a verb denotes time. For example, 'they have left' suggests an action that is complete, 'they are leaving' suggests an ongoing action and 'they will leave' suggests an action in the future.

assertion 99
An assertion is a forceful declaration that something is true, right or factually accurate when this may not necessarily be the case.

code 5
A language variety in which grammar and/or vocabulary are particular to a specific group.

cohesion 25
A term which refers to the patterns of language created within a text, mainly within and across sentence boundaries, and which collectively make up the organisation of larger units of text. Cohesion can be both lexical and grammatical. Lexical cohesion can be established by chains of words of related meaning which link across sentences (see also **semantic field**). Grammatical cohesion is established in a number of ways, including reference terms such as 'the', 'this', 'it' and so on.

comparative (see **degree**)

rhetorical question 52

A statement that is made in the form of a question, but which does not expect an answer.

semantic field 75

A group of words that are related in meaning as a result of being connected with a particular context of use.

soundbite 37

A short extract from a recorded speech or interview which is chosen because of its impact.

superlative (see **degree**)

synecdoche 26

The use of part of something to refer to the whole.

syntax 86

This refers to the organisation of sentence structure.

tag question 98

Tags are strings of words which are normally added to a declarative statement and which turn the statement into a question. For example, 'That was a good speech, *wasn't it?*'

transitivity 30

Transitivity involves looking at the language used to describe what happens, who are the participants (both those who do something and those affected by what is done), and what the circumstances are. This can lead to the attribution of blame or credit.

voice 30

Voice is a grammatical feature which indicates whether a subject in a sentence is the agent of an action or is affected by the action. Voice can normally be either active or passive. For example:

The Chancellor has raised taxes (active)
Taxes were raised by the Chancellor (passive)

The role of the Chancellor is emphasised more in the active sentence than in the passive. The passive voice also allows the 'by-phrase' to be omitted, thus deleting any reference to the agent:

Taxes were raised.

In this case responsibility for the action is concealed.

references

Atkinson, M. (1984) *Our Masters' Voices* (Methuen, London)

Ayer, A.J. (1936) *Language, Truth and Logic* (Gollancz, London)

Cockcroft, R. and Cockcroft, S.M. (1992) *Persuading People* (Macmillan, London)

Comfort, N. (1993) *Brewer's Politics* (Cassell, London)

Davies, P. (1997) *This England* (Little, Brown and Co., London)

Gibbs, R.W. (1994) *The Poetics of Mind* (Cambridge University Press, Cambridge)

Goatly, A. (1997) *The Language of Metaphors* (Routledge, London)

Lakoff, G. and Johnson, M. (1980) *Metaphor We Live By* (University of Chicago Press, Chicago)

Orwell, G. (1946) *Politics and the English Language* (Reprinted in *Inside the Whale and Other Essays*, Penguin, London, 1962)

Wilson, J. (1990) *Politically Speaking* (Blackwell, Oxford)

9 780415 201780